Thinking Styles

Thinking Styles

Robert J. Sternberg
Yale University

CAMBRIDGE
UNIVERSITY PRESS

PUBLISHED BY THE PRESS SYNDICATE OF THE UNIVERSITY OF CAMBRIDGE
The Pitt Building, Trumpington Street, Cambridge

CAMBRIDGE UNIVERSITY PRESS
The Edinburgh Building, Cambridge, United Kingdom
40 West 20th Street, New York, NY 10011-4211, USA
10 Stamford Road, Oakleigh, Melbourne 3166, Australia

First published 1997
First paperback edition 1999

Printed in the United States of America

Library of Congress Cataloging-in-Publication Data is available.

A catalog record for this book is available from the British Library.

ISBN 0 521 55316 4 hardback
ISBN 0 521 65713 X paperback

To my children, Seth and Sara, who have taught me more useful things about styles than has anyone else, and to whom I hope I have taught some useful things as well.

Contents

Preface

I've attended and been graduated from five schools: Tuscan Elementary, Maplewood Junior High School, Columbia High School, Yale College, and Stanford University. I performed better in each new school than I did in the old one – sometimes a little better, other times a lot better, but always better. At the same time, I've observed other people go through their own sequence of schools, and do a little worse in each new school. We were not unusual: Some students do a bit worse each time around, others a bit better, and still others no different from the last time around. Is it random? No. Is it more (or less) effort each new time around? No. What is it?

In our society, the first explanation that would come to anyone's mind would probably be abilities. Here, we see the educational system as a huge funnel; but this is a peculiar funnel, because it has a series of filters inside that allow fewer people to pass through each successive stage. Each filter, representing a school, has a different fineness of mesh. Highly selective schools are very fine-mesh filters that will let only the prime students through; slightly less selective schools are medium-mesh filters that will allow the choice students through as well; and even less selective schools are coarse filters that will allow successively less able students to get through.

Abilities do not explain the phenomenon I'm talking about. If we thought in terms of funnels with filters, then we would expect almost every student to do a bit worse at each next stage of career than at the last stage of career, as the funnel becomes narrower or the filter finer.

Such an explanation would not account for improved performance as the funnel narrows or the filter becomes finer. But many students do improve.

There is another explanation, and it has to do with thinking styles – how we prefer to use the abilities we have. People will do better or worse at successive stages of schooling and career as the environment provides a better or worse match to people's styles of thought. In this book, I will argue that thinking styles are as important as, and arguably more important than, abilities, no matter how broadly abilities are defined. Thus, constructs of social, practical, and emotional intelligence, or of multiple intelligences, expand our notions of what people *can do* – but the construct of style expands our notion of what people *prefer to do* – how they capitalize on the abilities they have. When your profile of thinking styles is a good match to an environment, you thrive. When it is a bad match, you suffer. Different levels of schooling and different subject areas reward different styles, with the result that you can do better or worse as you go through school (or jobs or relationships, for that matter), depending on how your profile of styles matches up with what the environment expects and on how the environment evaluates you. Similarly, different careers and levels of careers reward different styles differently. This book will be about styles and how they match up to different environments.

The book is divided into three main parts. Part I is about the proposed theory of styles and identifies and describes 13 important thinking styles. Part II presents the major principles of thinking styles and suggests how they originate and develop in people. Part III deals with styles of thinking and learning in the classroom, alternative theories, and what I perceive to be the advantages of the proposed theory.

The collaboration of a number of people has been indispensable in the development of this book. My first collaborator on styles, Marie Martin, worked with me to develop the first version of a *Thinking Styles Inventory*. Richard Wagner helped refine this instrument and collected some of the normative data for the refinement. I rely heavily on this refined instrument in describing the styles throughout the book, and in providing readers with self-assessments they can use. Elena Grigorenko further refined existing measures and also developed new measures.

She also was collaboratively involved in several of the studies described in the book, and is a coauthor of the paper on which Chapter 8 is based. My children, to whom this book is dedicated, helped me to understand styles, as did all my graduate and undergraduate advisees during the years I have taught at Yale. I am grateful to my wife, Alejandra Campos, for her unflagging support of me, and to my editor at Cambridge, Julia Hough, for supporting me in all phases of this project. Sai Durvasula helped in manuscript preparation.

Preparation of this book was supported by Grant R206R50001 from the U.S. Office of Educational Research and Improvement. The statements made in this book do not, however, necessarily reflect the positions of this office or of the United States government.

PART I

The Nature of Thinking Styles

1

What Are Thinking Styles and Why Do We Need Them?

When Susan was in the third grade, her teacher had a neat idea. The children were studying the planets, and the teacher wanted her students to learn actively, not just passively. So she decided to have the children pretend to be astronauts, and simulate going to Mars.

PENALIZING PEOPLE WHO DON'T FIT IN

This idea was a good one for promoting learning. What better way is there to learn about a place than to simulate being there, whether it be Mars, Venice, or Hoboken, for that matter? Here, the children would have to think about the air supply, the gravity, the terrain, and anything else that a visitor to Mars would have to consider. Of course, the children could learn all these things by reading about them. But their learning and their retention would certainly be enhanced by pretending to deal with them at first hand. However, they would have to know enough about Mars to be able to imagine being there. Reading would give the children an additional way to learn, and thus further enhance the learning process. But it could never be a substitute for the children's actively putting themselves in the place of astronauts.

As the children were preparing to be astronauts, Susan had an idea. How about if she dressed up as a Martian, and met the astronauts when they arrived on Mars? The teacher's idea was good, but perhaps Susan's was even better. For one thing, we do need to consider what it might be like if we ever actually encounter extraterrestrial aliens. But for another, all of us have to deal and cope with people who at times seem like extraterrestrial aliens, whether from Mars or from somewhere else.

If there is one thing I have learned in 20 years as a psychologist, it is that other people at times can seem to be incomprehensible, whether they be people from another culture or another social group, or even a spouse or lover. So what better preparation could there be for interacting with people who seem strange to us than to spend a few hours in the third grade thinking about what it would be like to interact with a Martian? Might as well get ready for the future, whatever it may hold.

When Susan told her idea to her teacher, the teacher immediately nixed it. Flustered, and perhaps needing a reason for her immediate no, the teacher patiently told Susan that we knew from space probes that there are no inhabitants of Mars, and so it would not be realistic to have Susan pretend to be a Martian. The teacher pointed out that she was doing a science lesson, and science lessons can't have nonexistent Martians in them.

The teacher's excuse was lame. For one thing, astronauts aren't going to Mars, either, not yet anyway. For another thing, space probes can't really assure us that there is no life on Mars: Maybe the Martians live in the interior of the planet, or maybe they exist as some life form that space probes cannot yet recognize. But these issues are only secondary to what made me so depressed when I heard about Susan's encounter with the teacher.

I began to wonder how many more times, when Susan had a creative idea, she would bother to express it, either to her teacher or to anyone else. I wondered how many times this same incident repeated itself, not only in Susan's classroom, or in the classroom of that teacher, but in countless classrooms at all grade levels and all around the world. How many punishments does it take for children to learn to suppress their creative ideas, and instead learn to play the school game? What's the game? Well, often it seems to be that if you have a creative idea, you should keep it to yourself. Unfortunately, schools are no worse than other institutions in playing such a game. Many families and many organizations play by the same rules.

It would be easy to jump on Susan's teacher and point out that there are bad apples in any profession. Easy, but wrong. Because what

Susan's teacher did, virtually every teacher, including myself, does at one time or another. After feeling myself become very hot under the collar upon hearing of the teacher's response, I cooled down pretty fast, because I realized that I was far from blameless myself. How many times had I been in a classroom, trying to teach too much material in too little time? I knew I had to finish the lesson that day and get on to the next one so that the students would be ready for the final exam, and later in their careers, possibly for the Psychology Advanced Test required for admission to many graduate schools.

Virtually all teachers operate under the same pressures: They need to teach to tests, and arguably, students who suppress their creativity will actually do better on most existing tests. The name of the test varies, but the fact of some test or another doesn't. The teacher is trying desperately to get through a lesson; it is going slower than it was supposed to because lessons hardly ever go exactly the way they are planned. Something that was supposed to be clear isn't, and a little more explanation is needed. Something else that was supposed to be easily explained isn't. And soon a 30-minute lesson becomes a 40- or 50-minute one. Then a student suggests a way of making a lesson that is going too slowly go even more slowly. The teacher's instantaneous reflex is to shoot a bullet – right through the student's idea, but also through the student's desire to be creative. The pattern repeats itself from time to time, from place to place, and eventually that student, and everyone else in the class who gets to watch, learns to play by the rules and to hide or suppress their creative ideas.

Let there be no doubt that most children do learn in school (just as most people learn on the job). But what do they learn? The most important lessons are often not those taught by the textbooks.

I have worked with both elementary-school students and with college students at Yale on developing ideas for experiments. The elementary-school students have an easier time of it. But when I ask the students to remember the details of or to critique already published studies – ones that are signed, sealed, and delivered – the Yale students win, hands down. The Yale students have developed the skills that schools value – the memory and analytical ones.

And what about the students who haven't learned? They pay – one way or another. Some are viewed as annoyances, or worse, as behavior problems. Others are viewed as show-offs. Still others come to be labeled as antisocial, and in many cases, start to fulfill the role that is suggested to them. Some teachers will tolerate these children; others won't. But few will appreciate them, because they disrupt what the teacher believes would otherwise be an orderly class. And orderly classes are easy-to-teach classes, whether the students are learning or not.

Organizations other than schools are little or no different. An organizational culture emerges that does things in a certain way. It has worked before. There is competitive pressure from all sides, so there is hardly enough time to produce what needs to be produced, much less to think about how it is being produced. People who question the way things are done are usually not viewed as creative, but rather as disruptive.

Several years ago we did a study of conceptions of intelligence, creativity, and wisdom in different occupations, one of which was business.[1] We asked participants in our study to rate a list of behaviors for how relevant they were to each of the attributes of intelligence, creativity, and wisdom. There was a negative correlation between ratings for conceptions of creativity and those for conceptions of wisdom. The behaviors that were seen as creative were viewed as unwise, and those that were seen as wise were viewed as uncreative.

The problem here might appear to be one of the individual who likes to think creatively in a school or other organization that discourages creativity, but the problem is more general than that – quite a bit more general. Consider the following situation.

LEARN MY WAY – OR ELSE

Ben is in his high school English class. The students are studying the *Odyssey,* one of the great works of Western literature, and certainly one from which any high school student has much to learn. But learn what? It is Parents' Day, and so Ben's parents are in the classroom. Ben's father knows that things have not been going well for his son in English that year, and he is about to find out why.

The teacher reads a quotation. Who said it? Here's another quotation. Who said this one? And here's another. Who said that? And what was happening at the time? And what happened next? Damned if Ben's father knows, but then, it's been more years than he cares to count since he has read the book. The level of detail that the teacher requires the students to remember seems to him quite extraordinary. Ben most definitely isn't a detail person. The whole class consists of remembering details of this order. The tests the teacher gives are the same: identifying who said what.

Ben's father talks to the teacher after the class, to ask what his goals are. The teacher explains that he is trying to teach the students to be able to read carefully. Makes sense. But does he have any other goals, the father asks him? The teacher replies that before students can start analyzing texts, they first have to learn to read them carefully. Before he starts analyzing texts, Ben will hate English, and not want to be bothered to analyze them. And all because the teacher has a model of learning that most psychologists realized to be wrong roughly 40 years ago.[2] His outdated model is not a function of his having gone to school in the stone age.[3] The teacher could not have been more than 30 years old. But the model is one he and many other teachers at all levels and of all subjects still accept. This incorrect model assumes that one should learn, *then* think, rather than that one should think to learn and thereby learn to think.

Ben also told his father that he doesn't like history. Why, the father asked? Ben's father loved history when he was Ben's age. Because he hates memorizing dates, Ben said. To Ben, learning history is synonymous with memorizing dates, just as learning English is synonymous with memorizing quotations. At least the teachers are consistent: The English teacher's tests consist primarily of quotations whose speakers are to be identified, and the history teacher's tests consist primarily of dates to be recalled.

So Ben learned to hate English and history. Some other student, who takes to memorizing quotes and dates, learns to like English and history. But there's a rub. Is the student who is good at learning "who said what" going to be the best writer or literary scholar? Is the student who is king of memorizing the dates of the reigns of various kings later going to be the best historian, or an ordinary citizen capable of using the past to understand the present? Perhaps not. The problem is not that the students had to learn facts: It's that that's all they were doing, and that the facts were being force-fed. The same thing is happening in millions of classrooms around the world.

Compare the stylistic demands of Ben's English class to those of his physics class for students of the same grade in the same school. The students were studying mass and its properties. The teacher had the students put on their coats and march outside. Once they were all outside, they made their way to the teacher's parking lot. The teacher divided the students into small groups, and then said: "This is my car. Your assignment today is to use the supplies I am going to give you to figure out the mass of my car." Students spent the entire class working in groups, interacting among themselves, and trying to figure out the mass of the teacher's car. Without doubt, the students who took to this assignment were in many cases not the same ones who took to the class of the English teacher. In fact, Ben loved the physics class, but hated the English class. As importantly, Ben's physics teacher admired him a great deal, his English teacher, not one whit.

There are two very general issues here, and they will be central themes of this book.

1. Schools and other institutions, from households to businesses to cultures, value certain ways of thinking more than others.
2. People whose ways of thinking do not match those valued by the institutions are usually penalized.

A *style* is a way of thinking. It is not an ability, but rather, a preferred way of using the abilities one has. The distinction between style and ability is a crucial one. An ability refers to how well someone can do something. A style refers to how someone likes to do something.

In our society, we think and talk a lot about abilities. Books such as Herrnstein and Murray's *The Bell Curve* show just how obsessed with abilities our society is.[4] And certainly abilities are important to success in school and later in life. Yet abilities are not and cannot be the whole story.

Although psychologists disagree regarding the predictive power of ability tests for various purposes, they all agree that they are highly imperfect predictors.[5] A consensus figure would be that tested differences in ability account for perhaps 20% of the variation among students in school performance, and 10% of the variation among workers in job performance. What about the rest of the variation – the 80% unexplained variation in school performance and the 90% unexplained variation in job performance? Thinking styles might be one source of unexplained variation. How people prefer to think might be just as important as how well they think. Consider three college roommates who illustrate this point.

THREE CASE STUDIES, THREE STYLES

The three college roommates had one thing in common: their high school records. All had been excellent students, and their Verbal and Mathematical SAT (Scholastic Assessment Test) scores were within a few points of each other. Even their patterns of abilities were the same: higher in verbal than in math, and definitely weak in spatial abilities. These were the kinds of people who could never get the suitcases to fit in the trunk of the car.

Alex was virtually a straight-A student in high school and had terrific test scores to boot. He was the kind of student every college wanted, and on April 15 of the fateful year for his application to colleges, he received many fat envelopes offering him acceptance. He went to an Ivy League college.

Alex's first three years were almost as distinguished as had been his high school years. He received mostly A's with a smattering of B's. He was considered one of the best. But then, his senior year, he had to do an independent project in his major, government. Alex liked to be given the structure within which he would work; and throughout his entire school career, he had been given this structure. His teachers had told him what to do, and he had done it, and done it well. Now, for the first time, there was no one to tell him what to do, and he was at loose ends. He was uncomfortable structuring the entire task himself, and it showed in the work he produced. He pulled a C on the project.

Alex has found a career that is a good match to his style of thinking. Today he is a contracts lawyer. Asked to describe his work, he explains that the investment bankers draw up the deal and decide what's to be what. Alex's job is to take their deal and set it down into a precisely written contract. Thus whereas Alex once took direction from his teachers, today he takes direction from the bankers. Alex explains that, to him, the ideal contract is one that is so perfect, so airtight, that if the bankers want to change their deal, they have to pay him to do it. In other words, they have to pay Alex every time they change their ideas. Little wonder that Alex has been so successful in his career: He's found a way to make his clients pay not only when they make up their minds about what to do, but also every time they change their minds.

Bill also had a strong high school record, although not as strong as Alex's. Bill liked to do things his own way, and so came into conflict with the constraints that any school imposed. Bill recognized that, to succeed, he would need to do well in school – and he did. But his major energy was devoted to his love, biology. He was involved in summer programs in biology, and did high-level research in biology even as a high school student. Moreover, his research was his own, not someone else's.

Bill's grades during his first three years of college were good, although not as good as Alex's. But his senior year, he and Alex crossed paths. Given the opportunity to do an independent senior thesis, Bill was in his element. He was now doing exactly what he had always most liked to do. And he received an A on the project, as well as an award for it.

Bill went on to graduate school to become a biologist, and today he is a successful researcher. His career is about as different from Alex's as another career could be. Bill, like Alex, loves his work, but for exactly the opposite reason. Whereas Alex likes translating the bankers' ideas into contract language, Bill likes translating his own ideas into language that is meaningful to biologists and laypeople alike. He is a team leader, and gives rather than takes direction.

Note that both Alex and Bill are very successful at what they do, but for different reasons. Neither would do well in the other's occupation, but not for lack of ability: Alex has the ability to be a biologist, Bill to be a lawyer. Rather, what makes them successful, given the basic ability to succeed, is that they are in jobs that are good matches to their styles of thinking. The same is true for Corwin.

Corwin went to the same Ivy League school as did Alex and Bill. He was quite critical of the school, as he tends to be of almost everything and everyone, himself not excepted. Indeed, Corwin is difficult to take in large doses because he is so critical. And because he is bright, his criticisms are usually on target. As a college student, Corwin wrote critiques of student productions, a task that fit him admirably.

Corwin's critical eye was not fixated only on courses. When he would go out on dates, Corwin would give his dates a test of values. The test was what is called a "nonobtrusive measurement": The dates never knew they were taking a test. But they most definitely were. If the woman passed, Corwin would go out with her again; if not, that was the end of that relationship.

Perhaps unsurprisingly, Corwin's relationships tended to be short-lived. No one quite met his standards. Today, Corwin is in his mid-fifties and still unmarried. I don't know if he is still giving the same test, or a variant of it. What I do know is that he has found a job that is a good match to his critical, judgmental style: Today, Corwin is a psychiatrist, and a good one. He spends his days evaluating patients and their problems, and prescribing and then administering treatment for them. He is very successful, as would befit someone who seems to like nothing more in life than to evaluate people and their problems.

The cases of Alex, Bill, and Corwin show us how styles can help us understand why, given equal abilities, one person chooses one career and another person chooses some other career. People with different styles like to use their abilities in different ways, and so respond differentially well to the kinds of thinking required in different occupations. Styles also help us understand why some people succeed in their chosen careers and others don't. Put Bill in Alex's career, and he is likely to find himself with no clients. He wants to do things his way, not the way of his clients. Put Alex in Bill's career, and the match will be equally bad: Alex prefers to be given direction. People need to find careers that match not only their abilities, but their styles as well.

THE IMPORTANCE OF MATCH BETWEEN STYLES AND ENVIRONMENTS

I care about styles, and you should too – if you care about your children, your spouse or lover, your colleagues at work, or yourself, for that matter. As a society, we repeatedly confuse styles with abilities, resulting in individual differences that are really due to styles being viewed as due to abilities. The result is that people whose styles don't match the expectations of their parents, spouse or lover, colleagues, or boss are derogated for all the wrong reasons. What is seen as stupidity or intransigence may actually be nothing more than a mismatch between the style of one individual and the style of another. Such mismatches become particularly serious when they occur in school or work settings.

In school, children who are viewed as stupid often suffer from nothing more than a style that mismatches that of their teacher. I know: When I took my introductory psychology course as a freshman in college, I was already eager to major in psychology. As a child, I had done extremely poorly on intelligence tests because of crippling test anxiety. The result was an interest in understanding intelligence that has not subsided to this day. Thus I took the introductory psychology course with every intention of using it as a launching point for a college major in psychology and later a career in the same field.

Those hopes came to an abrupt end when I got my grade for the course, a C. I first realized things were going badly when the professor handed us back our very first test result. It was an essay test, scored on a scale from 1 to 10. For some perverse reason, the professor had decided to hand back the test booklets in descending order of score. By the time I received mine, the only people left in the room were either a whole lot taller than I was, a whole lot heavier, or both. They, at least, were in college for a reason – in large part to play sports. It was no longer so clear why I was there. Indeed, I inferred that my own test booklet must have gotten out of order. But no, I received a 3 out of 10.

It turned out that what the professor expected from our essays and what I had thought he expected had no overlap. I thought that the use of an essay test meant the professor wanted us to be creative and go beyond the information given. In fact, the teacher had 10 points he wanted us to make about the topic of the essay. The test was scored on a 0 to 10 scale, depending upon the number of points that the professor wanted us to make that we actually had made. No pretenses about creativity; no attempt even to encourage critical thinking. And most certainly an atomic bomb dropped on a psychology career if ever I had seen one. Indeed, I even remember, perhaps falsely, a comment by the professor to the effect that there was one Sternberg in psychology already, and that it appeared that there would not soon be two. I got the message.

Fortunately, I decided to major in math. When I did even worse in math than I had done in psychology, I realized that psychology didn't look so bad after all, and I returned to the psychology major. In fact, I did well in my psychology courses after the introductory one. But I was one of the lucky ones, because I moved to a major in which I did even worse than I had done in psychology. How many other students, after bombing the introductory course in whatever they had thought was to be their life career, then switched to another major and had the misfortune to do pretty well in it?

For example, had I decided to switch to practically any subject except math – anthropology, sociology, English, history, biology, or whatever – I probably would have done well enough in the introductory course to pursue the major. I then would have ended up majoring in something that was interesting enough, but not what I really wanted to study. Countless students probably end up in this position, studying something that they like well enough, but that is not what they love, because they or others believe these students lack the ability to study what really interests them.

What's worse, we have the same situation here that we had with Ben's English class. The styles of thinking, and even the thinking abilities needed to succeed in the class, have little or nothing to do with the styles and abilities needed to succeed in the career. Since becoming a psychologist, I have not once had to memorize a book or a lecture, which is what I would have had to do to get an A in that introductory psychology course, and many other introductory courses as well, whether at the college or the secondary-school level. So what happens, exactly?

We reward and select into many fields – whether psychology or anything else – students who are good memorizers, but who will not necessarily think in ways that are compatible with the requirements of the jobs that a given field offers. At the same time, we derail students who may think in ways that are fully compatible with the career, but not with the requirements of the introductory course. In other words, we take in students who do not fit particularly well the demands of the career, and throw out students who do.

This sorting process is not just hypothetical. In our own graduate programs at Yale, one frequently hears professors talking about students who were straight-A students in college, and whose main talent in graduate school is, once again, getting straight A's. But at the graduate level, grades just don't matter a lot. Indeed, most institutions hiring doctoral or even masters level graduates don't care much about grades; many don't even require the transcript of course grades. What they are looking for are good psychologists or physicists or biologists or literary scholars or business executives or historians or whatever. And they know that good work in these fields has little to do with course grades.

At the same time, how many students were derailed from advanced training in their field of interest, who really might have made excellent psychologists or physicists or economists or whatever? In my estimation, quite a few. The styles for which we select are often not those that lead to success in a given field.

The problem I encountered in psychology is in no way limited to psychology. Consider a very different field, foreign languages. When I studied French in high school, I learned it by what is sometimes called the mimic-and-memorize method. You hear or see a phrase, and then you repeat it. Then you hear or see a variation of that phrase, and you repeat the variation. You repeat countless variations until you learn the varied ways in which a phrase can be transformed, and eventually you start building up a repertoire of phrases you can use when communicating in the language. This method benefits people whose styles lead them to want to be given a structure within which to work, and in particular, to memorize.

I wasn't a C student in French, but I was no genius either. Indeed, one day my teacher commented that he was interested in listening to the mistakes I made in French, because they showed that although I was doing reasonably well in the course, I was doing well by virtue of my general ability, not my foreign-language-learning aptitude. The mistakes sounded just horrible in French, and if I had the language aptitude, he commented, I would never use such horrible-sounding expressions.

I took what my teacher said to heart, and never took even one foreign-language course in college, or in graduate school, for that matter. After all, why risk a lousy grade when I wanted to go on to a successful career? Like many other college students, I inferred (probably correctly) that it wouldn't take more than a few low grades to reduce my chances of being admitted to the graduate program of my choice. I didn't want to spoil my chances for admission by taking courses that I didn't even really need.

Later it turned out that I really could have used some foreign-language courses. As an assistant professor of psychology, I received a call one day asking me whether I would be interested in meeting the minister for the development of intelligence of Venezuela. At the time, Venezuela was embarking on a unique enterprise in the history of the world: the creation of a government ministry that would be responsible for the development of the intelligence of the people of the country. The minister wanted me to do one of the projects that would soon be installed in the country's schools.

The challenge was so exciting, there was no way I was going to turn him down. There was just one rub. I was being asked to write a text to teach thinking skills to Spanish-speaking students who would be taught by Spanish-speaking teachers in a Spanish-speaking country. I used some of that general ability that my French teacher recognized to infer that it would be a good idea to learn some Spanish. And so I hired a graduate-student tutor to teach me some Spanish.

To my amazement, I learned Spanish easily and quickly, and enjoyed it much more than I had ever enjoyed French. It wasn't that the language was so different, or even really that my tutor was so much better as a teacher than my high school French teacher. Rather, the difference was the method by which I was taught.

The Spanish tutor used what is sometimes called the direct method, or the method of learning by context. I learned Spanish in the natural written and oral contexts in which it occurs. By reading and listening to actual dialogues, I inferred the meanings of the words from context. This way of learning well suited my preferred style of thinking – which is to create within real-world contexts – whereas the way of learning French had not. The result was that I learned Spanish quickly and French slowly.

Today I am a fluent Spanish speaker, but only a halting speaker of

French. I realize that I am neither more nor less talented in learning foreign languages than are other people. But like others, I learn better in some ways and worse in others. Once again, what we attribute to ability is really in part a question of styles of thinking and learning. It has to be: Students in Holland, Belgium, and many other countries around the world easily learn one, two, or more foreign languages, and no one thinks twice about it. Dutch and Belgian students are no smarter than American or British ones. Rather, they are taught in ways that better suit their styles of thinking and learning, and they are motivated to learn foreign languages in a way that our students almost never are.

Consider one final and very different example: the kind of quantitative thinking required to learn statistics. I have taught, from time to time, an advanced statistics course called multivariate analysis. For a number of years, I brought all my advanced training and research on the diversity of abilities to bear upon this class in a thoughtful and sophisticated way. I classified my students into two groups: the smarts and the dumbs!

The smarts could do almost nothing wrong. They understood the material quickly, did their homework with little difficulty, and did well on tests. The dumbs could do practically nothing right. They seemed only minimally to understand the material in class. They had great difficulty completing the homework assignments. And their test scores reflected their general lack of understanding of the material. Nothing complicated here, or so I thought.

One year, I was reading a book that presented many of the statistical techniques that I had been teaching in a geometric rather than an algebraic fashion. I had always taught the course algebraically, requiring students to derive, understand, and apply formulas, and requiring them to see the relations among the equations that constituted the basic formulas of multivariate data analysis. After reading the book, I decided to try an experiment, namely, to teach a class that I had just taught algebraically one more time, but this time presenting the very same material geometrically.

The results were astonishing. Many of the students who were consigned to the garbage heap of the "dumb" classification suddenly understood what I was saying perfectly well. It was as though they had become different people. Simultaneously, many of the students who had quickly and easily followed the algebraic presentations stumbled when I presented the material geometrically. I'm embarrassed to say that it wasn't only students who stumbled. I am not a geometric thinker, and I needed some of the students – some of the "dumber" students, that is – to correct me at various points in the lecture. And I realized that day that over the years, many of the students that I had thought to be dumb were not stupid at all, but rather simply did not learn in a way that was compatible with the way I was teaching. But my teaching the material in just a single way had never even given them a chance.

There is a lesson to be learned here, and the lesson is nothing complicated. Many of the students we are consigning to the dust heaps of our classrooms have the abilities to succeed. It is we, not they, who are failing. We are failing to recognize the variety of thinking and learning styles they bring to the classroom, and teaching them in ways that don't fit them well.

The same principle applies to employees. I hired an employee as a clerical assistant. She was bright, but had little background in psychology or research. The job she was in required her to do clerical work in a fairly set way and according to a certain routine. She kept coming up with new and, frankly, better ways of doing things. But sometimes, things needed to be done a certain way, even if it wasn't the best way, because of the way journals require articles to be submitted. Her ideas were innovative, but the journals weren't going to change their policies because she had better ideas.

Eventually, I realized she was being wasted on the clerical job. I put her into a research job, where coming up with better ways of testing hypotheses was an important part of the job. She not only learned research skills on the job, but was better at the work than many people with prior training. At times, her lack of training was, in fact, a problem. But I made the most of her stylistic preferences by putting her in a job that encouraged innovation rather than merely tolerating it.

I want to emphasize that I am no more innocent than any other teacher or employer. As I mentioned, for many years, I labeled as "stupid" students who could have learned statistics well, but in a way that was different from the way I was teaching it. Similarly, in introductory psychology, I was determined not to teach my own course the way my professor had taught me, and so I taught in a way that matched my styles of thinking and learning and that was totally unlike the course my professor had taught. In teaching this way, however, I simply moved the spotlight from one group of students to another.

Instead of favoring a group who enjoyed memorization and learning the facts, and, most of all, being told what to do, I favored a group who liked to create and go beyond the information given – students who wanted to do things their own way. Really, I was doing exactly what my own professor had done – favoring a group like myself to the exclusion of groups who weren't like me. It wasn't until I started taking seriously the issue of thinking and learning styles that I realized how important such consideration was to building success for all students into the curriculum.

The story is no different for those who have worked for me. I realized that instead of favoring those employees who had my own preferred thinking and learning styles, I needed to appreciate employees for what they had to offer. I needed to see them in their own terms, and thus help them make the most of their jobs and their personal lives. So let's now embark on an exploration – an exploration of thinking styles, and what an understanding of them has to offer us.

THINKING STYLES

Why do so many people who fail in school succeed in life, and vice versa? Why do some people turn to law, others to medicine, and still others to accounting? And why do some of those doctors who were straight-A students in medical school fail their patients? Why is it that some gifted kids get straight A's in school, whereas others with equal abilities flunk out? These are just some of the questions that can be addressed through an understanding of styles of thinking.

My thesis in this book is that what happens to us in life depends not just on *how well* we think, but also on *how* we think. People think in different ways, and moreover, our research has shown that they over-estimate the extent to which others think the way they do. As a result, misunderstandings can develop – between spouses, parents and children, teachers and students, and bosses and employees. Understanding styles of thinking and learning can help people prevent these misunderstandings, and actually come to a better understanding of each other and of themselves.

What Are Thinking Styles and Why Do We Need Them?

A style is a preferred way of thinking. It is not an ability, but rather how we use the abilities we have. We do not have *a* style, but rather a *profile* of styles. People may be practically identical in their abilities and yet have very different styles. But society does not always judge people with equal abilities as equal. Rather, people whose styles match those expected in certain situations are judged as having higher levels of abilities, despite the fact that what is present is not ability, but fit between those people's styles and the tasks they are confronting.

Often, the tasks people face could be arranged better to fit their styles, or they could modify their styles to fit the tasks. But if an attribution is made that the people do not have the requisite abilities, the people typically never even get a chance to change their approach.

Go to any high school or college reunion, and you will meet scores of people who went into the wrong job for themselves. They may have done what their guidance or career counselor told them to do, based on abilities or even interests. But many of them have found careers where they feel like they are at a dead end. Being at a dead end is often in the mind of the beholder, and one often feels at a dead end when the work one does is a misfit to the way in which one best uses the talents one has. Understanding styles can help people better understand why some activities fit them and others don't, and even why some people fit them and others don't.

Why a Theory of Mental Self-government?

The basic idea of the theory of mental self-government is that the forms of government we have in the world are not coincidental. Rather, they are external reflections of what goes on in people's minds. They represent alternative ways of organizing our thinking. Thus, the forms of government we see are mirrors of our minds.

There are a number of parallels between the organization of the individual and the organization of society. For one thing, just as society needs to govern itself, so do we need to govern ourselves. We need to decide on priorities, as does a government. We need to allocate our resources, just as does a government. We need to be responsive to changes in the world, as does a government. And just as there are obstacles to change in government, so are there obstacles to change within ourselves. Here is an overview of the proposed theory.

Functions of Mental Self-government

Roughly speaking, governments serve three functions: executive, legislative, and judicial. The executive branch carries out the initiatives, policies, and laws enacted by the legislative branch, and the judicial branch evaluates whether the laws are being carried out correctly and if there are violations of these laws. People also need to perform these functions in their own thinking and working.

Legislative people like to come up with their own ways of doing things, and prefer to decide for themselves what they will do and how they will do it. Legislative people like to create their own rules, and prefer problems that are not prestructured or prefabricated. In the examples cited earlier, Ben was a legislative stylist. Some of the preferred kinds of activities of a legislative stylist are writing creative papers, designing innovative projects, creating new business or educational systems, and inventing new things. Some of the kinds of occupations they prefer, all of which let them exercise their legislative bent, are creative writer, scientist, artist, sculptor, investment banker, policy maker, and architect.

The legislative style is particularly conducive to creativity, because creative people need not only the ability to come up with new ideas, but also the desire to. Unfortunately, school environments do not often reward the legislative style. Indeed, even the training for occupations that require people to be creative often discourages the legislative style. Thus, a person might find him- or herself in a science course, required to memorize facts, formulas, and charts. Yet scientists almost never have to memorize anything: If they don't remember something, they look it up on their bookshelf.

Creative writers also need a legislative style, but a legislative style is not often encouraged, and is often discouraged in literature classes, where the emphasis in the lower grades is likely to be on comprehension and in the upper grades on criticism and analysis.

Executive people like to follow rules and prefer problems that are prestructured or prefabricated. They like to fill in the gaps within existing structures rather than to create the structures themselves. Some of the kinds of activities they are likely to prefer are solving given mathematical problems, applying rules to problems, giving talks or lessons based on other people's ideas, and enforcing rules. Some occupations that can be a good fit to executive thinkers are certain types of lawyer, police officer on patrol, builder of other people's designs, soldier, proselytizer for other people's systems, and administrative assistant.

The executive style tends to be valued both in school and in business, because executive stylists do what they are told, and often do it cheerfully. They follow directions and orders, and evaluate themselves in the same way the system is likely to evaluate them, namely, in terms of how well they do what they are told. Thus, a gifted child with an executive style is likely to do well in school, whereas a gifted child with a legislative style is more likely to be viewed as nonconforming and even rebellious.

Peer-group pressure encourages children to adopt an executive style as well, but with respect to the norms of the peer group rather than of the school. Thus, pressure from many sources can lead students to adopt this style.

Judicial people like to evaluate rules and procedures, and prefer problems in which one analyzes and evaluates existing things and ideas. The judicial stylist likes activities such as writing critiques, giving opinions, judging people and their work, and evaluating programs. Some of their preferred kinds of occupations are judge, critic, program evaluator, consultant, admissions officer, grant and contract monitor, and systems analyst.

Schools often shortchange the judicial style. Although the work of a historian, for example, is in large part judicial – the analysis of historical events – many children get the idea that the work is largely executive – remembering dates of events. As in science, therefore, some of the ablest students may decide to pursue some other field, even though their style of thinking may be well suited not to their preparation for the career, but to the actual career itself.

Problems of mismatching are not limited to the school. In many businesses, including schools, lower-level managers are sought who have a largely executive style. They do what they are told, and try to do it well. People with such a style are often then promoted into the higher levels of management. The problem is that in the higher levels, a more legislative or judicial style also becomes desirable. But many of the people with a more legislative or judicial style may well have been derailed early in their management careers, so that they never get to the higher levels of management. People may be promoted to higher positions for which their styles are not suited. Small wonder, for example, that some school administrators are reluctant to accept change. They got to where they are because they did what they were told to do, not because they liked to decide what to do in the first place.

The Forms of Mental Self-government

The theory of mental self-government specifies four forms: monarchic, hierarchic, oligarchic, and anarchic. Each form results in a different way of approaching the world and its problems.

A *monarchic* person is someone who is single-minded and driven. The individual tends not to let anything get in the way of his or her solving a problem. Monarchic people can be counted on to get a thing done, given that they have set their mind to it.

Monarchic bosses often expect tasks to be done, without excuses or extenuating circumstances. When you get married to a monarchic individual, you usually find it out quickly. You may see little of the person, and when you do see the person, his or her mind may be elsewhere. If you, rather than, say, work, are the subject of a monarchic spouse's obsession, you may find yourself receiving more attention than you expected.

Monarchic children often encounter a problem in school: They usually want to be doing something other than what they are doing, and are likely to be thinking about the other thing while they are supposed to be attending to the teacher. Sometimes, their interests are best served when a teacher (or parent) brings whatever they are monarchic about to bear on other things they are doing. For example, a child who has a strong interest in sports but is not a reader may become a reader if given sports novels to read (as I did with my son). A child who loves cooking but not math could be given math problems to do that involve recipes. In these ways, the child may become interested in things that previously were of no interest.

The *hierarchic* person has a hierarchy of goals and recognizes the need to set priorities, as all goals cannot always be fulfilled, or at least fulfilled equally well. This person tends to be more accepting of complexity than is the monarchic person, and recognizes the need to view problems from a number of angles so as to set priorities correctly.

Hierarchic individuals tend to fit well into organizations because they recognize the need for priorities. However, if their priorities are different from those of the organization, problems may arise. Then they may find themselves organizing their work according to their own, but not their organization's, priorities. The company lawyer who wants to spend too much time on pro bono work, the university professor who wants to spend too much time teaching, and the cook who wants each meal to be perfect but who takes forever in cooking the meals may soon find themselves unwelcome in their respective organizations.

The *oligarchic* person is like the hierarchic person in having a desire to do more than one thing within the same time frame. But unlike hierarchic people, oligarchic people tend to be motivated by several, often competing goals of equal perceived importance. Often, these individuals feel pressured in the face of competing demands on their time and other resources. They are not always sure what to do first, or how much time to allot to each of the tasks they need to complete. However, given even minimal guidance as to the priorities of the organization in which they are involved, they can become as effective or even more effective than people with other styles.

The *anarchic* person seems to be motivated by a potpourri of needs and goals that can be difficult for him or her, as well as for others, to sort out. Anarchic people take what seems like a random approach to problems; they tend to reject systems, and especially rigid ones, and to fight back at whatever system they see as confining them.

Although anarchic individuals may have trouble adapting to the worlds of school and work, especially if the environment is a rigid one, they often have greater potential for creative contribution than do many of the people who find the anarchics so distasteful. Because anarchics tend to pick up a little from here, a little from there, they often put together diverse bits of information and ideas in a creative way. They are wide-ranging in the scope of things they will consider, and so may see solutions to problems that others overlook. The problem for the teacher, parent, or employer is to help the anarchic person harness this potential for creativity, and achieve the self-discipline and organization that are necessary for any kind of a creative contribution. If this harnessing effort works, then the anarchic person may end up succeeding in domains where others may fail.

LEVELS, SCOPE, AND LEANINGS OF MENTAL SELF-GOVERNMENT

Global individuals prefer to deal with relatively large and abstract issues. They ignore or don't like details, and prefer to see the forest rather than the trees. Often, they lose sight of the trees that constitute the forest. As a result, they have to be careful not to get lost on "Cloud Nine."

Local individuals like concrete problems requiring working with details. They tend to be oriented toward the pragmatics of a situation, and are down-to-earth. The danger is that they may lose the forest for the trees. However, some of the worst system failures, such as in aviation and rocketry, have occurred when people have ignored what seemed at the time to be small details. Thus, almost any team requires at least some local individuals.

Global and local people can work particularly well together, because each attends to an aspect of task completion that the other would rather forget. Two global people trying to complete a project may each want to deal with the big issues, leaving no one to attend to the details; two local people may find themselves without anyone to do the higher-order initial planning needed to get the job done. It helps if neither individual is so extreme that he or she cannot understand and appreciate what the other has to offer. Extreme localists or globalists can get carried away, and start to lose sight either that the big issues exist, or that there are details that someone needs to attend to.

Internal individuals are concerned with internal affairs – that is to say, these individuals turn inward. They tend to be introverted, task-oriented, aloof, and sometimes socially less aware. They like to work alone. Essentially, their preference is to apply their intelligence to things or ideas in isolation from other people.

An example of how teachers (or anyone else) can confuse style with abilities is shown by the case of a kindergartner who was recommended by her teacher for retention. When asked why she had made this recommendation, the teacher pointed out that although the child's academic work was quite good, the child did not seem "socially ready" for first grade. That is to say, the child preferred to be on her own rather than to interact with other children, which the teacher took as a lack of some kind of social intelligence. In fact, the child was simply an internal. She was promoted, and has done splendidly well both academically and in her social relations.

External individuals tend to be extroverted, outgoing, and people-oriented. Often, they are socially sensitive and aware of what is going on with others. They like working with other people wherever possible.

Many of the questions that arise in education as to "what is better?" stem from a fundamental misunderstanding of the interaction of styles with learning experience. For example, in recent years, there has been a strong push toward what is called "cooperative learning," which means children working together to learn in groups. The idea is supposed to be that children will learn better in small working groups than they will when they are left to their own devices.

From the standpoint of the theory of mental self-government, there is no single right answer to questions such as whether children learn better individually or in groups, and indeed, this question, like so many others, is viewed as misformulated. External children will prefer working in groups and will probably learn better when learning with others. Internal children will probably prefer to work alone, and may become anxious in a group setting.

This is not to say that internals should never work in groups, or externals, alone. Obviously, each kind of individual needs to develop the flexibility to learn to work in a variety of situations. But the stylistic nt of view implies that teachers, like students, need to be flexible in .... way they approach the teaching-learning process. They need to provide children with both individual and group settings so that children can be comfortable some of the time and challenged the rest of the time. Always providing the same working setting tends to benefit some students and to penalize others.

The *liberal* individual likes to go beyond existing rules and procedures, to maximize change, and to seek situations that are somewhat ambiguous. The individual is not necessarily "politically" liberal. A political conservative could have a liberal style in trying to implement, say, a Republican agenda in a new and all-encompassing way. Thrill-seekers tend to have a liberal style, as do people who, in general, quickly become bored.

The *conservative* individual likes to adhere to existing rules and procedures, minimize change, avoid ambiguous situations where possible, and stick with familiar situations in work and professional life. This individual will be happiest in a structured and relatively predictable environment. When such structure does not exist, the individual may seek to create it.

So, those are all the styles in the theory. The various styles are summarized below. In Chapters 2, 3, and 4, we will consider them in more detail.

Summary of Styles of Thinking

	Functions	Forms
	Legislative	Monarchic
	Executive	Hierarchic
	Judicial	Oligarchic
		Anarchic

Levels	Scope	Leanings
Global	Internal	Liberal
Local	External	Conservative

2

Functions of Thinking Styles

The Legislative, Executive, and Judicial Styles

Governments can be organized in many different ways, but all of them need to accomplish at least three different functions: They need to legislate; they need to execute the legislation they pass; and they need to judge whether the legislation is consistent with their principles, and if it is, whether people are acting in accord with the legislation.

Before presenting each style, I will first give you an opportunity to assess yourself on the style. Take the self-assessment before reading about the style. It will help you understand the style better, as well as to understand yourself better.

Because the instructions are the same for all the self-assessments in the book, the full instructions are given in advance here, and then just summarized for each individual self-assessment. Each of the self-assessments in this chapter and in Chapters 2 to 4 is from the Sternberg-Wagner Thinking Styles Inventory.[1]

Instructions for Stylistic Self-Assessment

Read each statement carefully and decide how well it describes you. Use the scale provided to indicate how well the statement fits the way you typically do things on the job, at home, or at school. Write 1 if the statement does *not* fit you at all, that is, you almost never do things this way. Write 7 if the statement fits you extremely well, that is, you almost always do things this way. Use the values in between to indicate that the statement fits you in varying degrees:

1 = Not at all well   4 = Somewhat well   6 = Very well
2 = Not very well   5 = Well   7 = Extremely well
3 = Slightly well

There are, of course, no right or wrong answers. Please read each statement and write next to the statement the scale number that best indicates how well the statement describes you. Proceed at your own pace, but do not spend too much time on any one statement.

THE LEGISLATIVE STYLE

Before reading on, start with Self-assessment 2.1. Then score yourself using the scoring system given at the end of the test.

Self-assessment 2.1. *Sternberg-Wagner Self-Assessment Inventory on the Legislative Style*

Read each of the following statements, and then rate yourself on a 1–7 scale, where each rating corresponds to how well a statement describes you: 1 = Not at all well; 2 = Not very well; 3 = Slightly well; 4 = Somewhat well; 5 = Well; 6 = Very well; and 7 = Extremely well.

___ 1. When making decisions, I tend to rely on my own ideas and ways of doing things.
___ 2. When faced with a problem, I use my own ideas and strategies to solve it.
___ 3. I like to play with my ideas and see how far they go.
___ 4. I like problems where I can try my own way of solving them.
___ 5. When working on a task, I like to start with my own ideas.
___ 6. Before starting a task, I like to figure out for myself how I will do my work.

— 7. I feel happier about a job when I can decide for myself what and how to do it.

— 8. I like situations where I can use my own ideas and ways of doing things.

Interpreting Scores

The way you evaluate your score is to add up the eight numbers you wrote down above, and then divide by 8. Carry out the division to one decimal place. You now should have a number between 1.0 and 7.0. There are six categories of scores, which depend on your status and your sex. These six categories are shown below.

Nonstudent Adults			
	Category	Male	Female
Very High	(Top 1%–10%)	6.6–7.0	6.5–7.0
High	(Top 11%–25%)	6.1–6.5	6.2–6.4
High Middle	(Top 26%–50%)	5.5–6.0	5.2–6.1
Low Middle	(Top 51%–75%)	4.9–5.4	4.5–5.1
Low	(Top 76%–90%)	4.3–4.8	3.6–4.4
Very Low	(Top 91%–100%)	1.0–4.2	1.0–3.5

College Student Adults			
	Category	Male	Female
Very High	(Top 1%–10%)	6.2–7.0	6.0–7.0
High	(Top 11%–25%)	5.6–6.1	5.6–5.9
High Middle	(Top 26%–50%)	5.1–5.5	5.1–5.5
Low Middle	(Top 51%–75%)	4.4–5.0	4.5–5.0
Low	(Top 76%–90%)	4.0–4.3	4.1–4.4
Very Low	(Top 91%–100%)	1.0–3.9	1.0–4.0

If you scored in the "very high" category, then you have all or almost all of the characteristics of a legislative person. If you scored in the "high" category, you have many of these characteristics. And if you scored in the "high middle" category, then you have at least some of the characteristics. If you scored in the bottom three categories, then this is not one of your preferred styles. Keep in mind, though, that just how legislative you are may vary across tasks, situations, and your time of life.

In a nutshell, legislative people like to do things their own way. They like creating, formulating, and planning things. In general, they tend to be people who like to make their own rules.

Sam is a new, entry-level manager in a traditional company in the Midwest that is well known for its breakfast cereals. The company is also known both for the quality of its products and for its traditional way of doing things. Although the company introduces new cereals from time to time, the way in which the cereals are introduced follows a set course. It is often joked that in order to be promoted, you have to have overseen the introduction of at least one new, unsuccessful breakfast cereal. Of course, failure rates for new breakfast cereals have always been high in every such company. But Sam believes he has some ideas about how to achieve a higher success rate. In an effort to impress upper management, he communicates and pushes for some of his new ideas. Unwittingly, Sam places himself on the path to managerial derailment. He's a legislative thinker in a company that does not value legislative thinking in its mid-level managers. He defies the corporate culture, which in turn ditches him.

With children, it is sometimes necessary to remind them that no one gets to be "legislative" all the time. Legislative students tend to be critical of the schooling they receive, often justly so. They may not want to do things the ways their teachers want them to. It is important to remind them that no system can function without some rules and set procedures, even if the rules and procedures are suboptimal. In the case of my own legislative son, I remind him to avoid the small, unimportant skirmishes with the school and to save himself for the major battles. Otherwise, he'll lose credibility, as well as the skirmishes.

Legislative people enjoy doing things the way they decide to do them. They prefer problems that are not prestructured for them, but rather that they can structure for themselves. This tendency can be costly in many school environments. It also is not compatible with the format of many examinations and standardized tests in the United States. In this country, you can go around to college bookstores and find some of them selling answer sheets for electronically scored standardized tests. Students not only have to study for and take the tests; they have to pay extra to buy the response sheets on which to make their black marks or circles. Contrast the U.S. system to that of universities in England such as Oxford or Cambridge, where there are no multiple-choice tests at all, and where students' examinations are all in the form of essays. According to Maryanne Martin of the psychology department at Oxford, evaluators encourage and grade higher essays that show innovative and fresh thinking – in other words, that show the legislative style. The legislative student who might get a highly coveted First degree in England at a university such as Oxford might very well get a C in an American university, simply because of the difference in the kinds of styles valued by the tests.

Legislative people also prefer creative and constructive planning-based activities, such as writing papers, designing projects, and creating new business or educational systems. Often, very successful entrepreneurs succeed precisely because they are legislative and want to create their own way of doing things. Steve Jobs and Steve Wozniak, the founders of Apple Computer, were good examples of such a stylistic preference. But when companies become more entrenched and need a more stable form of management, entrepreneurs are often not at their best. Not atypically, a new cadre of managers emerges, as happened at Apple. Sometimes, this new cadre later runs into problems itself, when times start to change rapidly, and they, indifferent or perhaps even averse to the legislative style, do not.

Remember Susan, described in Chapter 1? In suggesting to her teacher that she dress up like a Martian, she was showing a legislative style. The teacher basically told her to shut up, and the lesson here, as so often for legislative students as well as employees, is that if you have an idea about the way things might be done, keep quiet about it. Bill, the college student described in Chapter 1, also showed a legislative style.

On the whole, legislative people have certain likes and dislikes. Table 2.1 shows some of their typical likes and dislikes. A second way you can gauge yourself is to see whether your own preferences correspond more to the likes (high legislative) or the dislikes (low legislative).

In part because of these likes and dislikes, legislative people tend to adapt particularly well, on the whole, to certain occupations. Examples

Table 2.1. *Likes and Dislikes of Legislative-Creators*

Likes	Dislikes
In School	
Writing creative essays	Writing essays that recite facts or a teacher's point of view
Writing short stories	Summarizing short stories of others
Writing poems	Memorizing poems
Writing alternative endings to existing stories	Remembering the individual events in existing stories
Inventing math problems	Solving math problems in books
Designing science projects	Doing science experiments where the steps are prepackaged
Writing about possible future events	Recounting past events
Putting self in the position of a famous historical personage	Remembering the birth and death dates of a famous historical personage
Drawing an original work of art of one's own choice	Drawing one's house or car or whatever one is told to draw
On the Job	
Deciding on what work to do	Being told what work to do
Giving orders	Receiving orders
Deciding on company policy	Being told to follow company policy
Designing systems for getting work done	Implementing preexisting systems for getting work done
Deciding whom to hire	Orienting hired people according to company policy
At Home	
Deciding what kind of food to eat and where to eat	Carrying out the already decided-on eating arrangements
Deciding where to go Saturday night	Arranging to get to the place where your partner has decided to go Saturday night
Deciding whom to invite to a party	Preparing and sending the party invitations
Deciding on limits for the kids	Enforcing the limits for the kids
Plotting the route for the family vacation	Getting the family to the vacation destination in one piece

of occupations they typically like are novelist, playwright, poet, mathematician, scientist, architect, inventor, fashion designer, policy maker, entrepreneur, composer, choreographer, and advertising creative copywriter.

In schools as well as at work, legislative people are often viewed as not fitting in, or perhaps as annoying. They want to do things their own way, which more often than not does not correspond to the way of the institution. In an organization that has a fixed way of doing things and expects its members to do things in that way, the legislator has no respected place. In a school where teachers give fixed assignments and may have a rigid idea of what constitutes a good performance on those assignments, the legislative student may come out looking either not very bright or possibly disruptive.

THE EXECUTIVE STYLE

Before reading about the executive style, be sure to take Self-assessment 2.2. Then score yourself using the normative data that follow the quiz.

Self-assessment 2.2. *Sternberg-Wagner Self-Assessment Inventory on the Executive Style*

Read each of the following statements, and then rate yourself on a 1–7 scale, where each rating corresponds to how well a statement describes you: 1 = Not at all well; 2 = Not very well; 3 = Slightly well; 4 = Somewhat well; 5 = Well; 6 = Very well; and 7 = Extremely well.

___ 1. When discussing or writing down ideas, I follow formal rules of presentation.

___ 2. I am careful to use the proper method to solve any problem.

___ 3. I like projects that have a clear structure and a set plan and goal.

___ 4. Before starting a task or project, I check to see what method or procedure should be used.

___ 5. I like situations in which my role or the way I participate is clearly defined.

___ 6. I like to figure out how to solve a problem following certain rules.

___ 7. I enjoy working on things that I can do by following directions.

___ 8. I like to follow definite rules or directions when solving a problem or doing a task.

Interpreting Scores

The way you evaluate your score is to add up the eight numbers you wrote down above, and then divide by 8. Carry out the division to one decimal place. You now should have a number between 1.0 and 7.0. There are six categories of scores, which depend on your status and your sex. These six categories are shown below.

Nonstudent Adults			
	Category	Male	Female
Very High	(Top 1%–10%)	6.0–7.0	5.8–7.0
High	(Top 11%–25%)	5.3–5.9	5.3–5.7
High Middle	(Top 26%–50%)	4.5–5.2	4.4–5.2
Low Middle	(Top 51%–75%)	3.6–4.4	3.4–4.3
Low	(Top 76%–90%)	2.9–3.5	2.7–3.3
Very Low	(Top 91%–100%)	1.0–2.8	1.0–2.6

College Student Adults			
	Category	Male	Female
Very High	(Top 1%–10%)	5.5–7.0	5.1–7.0
High	(Top 11%–25%)	5.0–5.4	4.9–5.0
High Middle	(Top 26%–50%)	4.2–4.9	4.2–4.8
Low Middle	(Top 51%–75%)	3.6–4.1	3.7–4.1
Low	(Top 76%–90%)	3.1–3.5	3.1–3.6
Very Low	(Top 91%–100%)	1.0–3.0	1.0–3.0

If you scored in the "very high" category, then you have all or almost all of the characteristics of an executive person. If you scored in the "high" category, you have many of these characteristics. And if you scored in the "high middle" category, then you have at least some of the characteristics. If you scored in the bottom three categories, then this is not one of your preferred styles. Keep in mind, though, that just how executive you are may vary across tasks, situations, and your time of life.

Basically, people with the executive style are implementers: They like to do, and generally prefer to be given guidance as to what to do or how to do what needs to be done. They are like Alex, the contracts lawyer, described in the vignette in Chapter 1. These are people who like to follow rules. Executive people can often tolerate the kinds of bureaucracies that drive more legislative people batty.

Sharon and Beatrice were both mid-level directors in an agency of the federal government. They started working at the same time. Their jobs both pertained to program management in different aspects of health care. Sharon's style was primarily legislative, Beatrice's, executive. Sharon had lots of ideas for improving the functioning of the agency and was eager to implement them; Beatrice had some ideas of her own, but was willing to work within the system and see her ideas introduced gradually, and in some cases, not at all.

Three years after they started work, some of Beatrice's ideas, but none of Sharon's, had been implemented. One more year and Sharon was on the job market, frustrated and burned out. Unable to adapt to the bureaucratic environment, she saw her rather revolutionary ideas thwarted at every turn. Beatrice, in contrast, was willing to take direction, which resulted in her superiors' being more willing to listen to her and to make changes when she suggested evolutionary rather than revolutionary modifications to procedure. Ironically, therefore, it is not always the legislative person who gets his or her way, especially in a bureaucratic environment.

Executive people also like to enforce rules and laws (their own or others'). A major part of my own job is writing proposals to government and private granting agencies. The requests for proposals seem to have been made to order for executive proposers, because there are so many rules to be followed. What's a primarily legislative person to do? After once having a proposal sent back because one of an infinite number of forms was not properly filled out, I started asking my assistant to handle issues of compliance. People compensate for styles they do not prefer by collaborating with others who do prefer those styles.

Executive people prefer problems that are given to them or structured for them and like to be and take pride in being doers – in getting things done. It is for this reason that legislative-executive teams can be so successful. The legislative person often gets his or her satisfaction out of proposing, the executive person, out of getting done what was in the proposal. The two kinds of people thus well complement each other.

Collaboration is not always possible, and so individuals may have to "redefine" what they are doing in order to motivate themselves. Legislative scientists or others scholars, for example, are often more interested in formulating research than they are in what they may see as the more banal process of writing the research up. But they may succeed in getting their material written up if they look at the writing as a creative challenge rather than just as a mundane rendering of the facts. Similarly, executive people may motivate themselves to do proposals for projects if they realize that the proposals, which they do not like writing, are short-term inconveniences in the service of the process of actually doing the long-term project.

Executive people tend to gravitate toward occupations that are quite different from those to which legislative people are attracted. Some of the occupations executive people tend to like are police officer, soldier, teacher, administrator, applied researcher who is given problems to work on by management, driver, firefighter, and certain types of medical doctor. Their pattern of likes and dislikes is essentially the opposite of that of legislative people.

Executive people will tend to be valued by organizations that want people to do things in a way that adheres to a set of rules or guidelines. Who will best fill a position often depends on the stylistic norms to which the holder of that position is expected to adhere. For example, boards of education typically select superintendents. A board that wants someone who takes direction from them will be happiest with an executive person in the position of superintendent, whereas a board that wants someone who takes a ball and runs with it in his or her own direction will be happiest with a legislative person. This example shows how, although jobs may seem to require styles, it is actually how performance is evaluated in those jobs that can determine who "best" fits the job.

THE JUDICIAL STYLE

Before reading on, start with Self-assessment 2.3. Then score yourself using the scoring system at the end of the test.

Self-assessment 2.3 *Sternberg-Wagner Self-Assessment Inventory on the Judicial Style*

Read each of the following statements, and then rate yourself on a 1–7 scale, where each rating corresponds to how well a statement describes you: 1 = Not at all well; 2 = Not very well; 3 = Slightly well; 4 = Somewhat well; 5 = Well; 6 = Very well; and 7 = Extremely well.

____   1. When discussing or writing down ideas, I like criticizing others' ways of doing things.
____   2. When faced with opposing ideas, I like to decide which is the right way to do something.
____   3. I like to check and rate opposing points of view or conflicting ideas.
____   4. I like projects where I can study and rate different views and ideas.
____   5. I prefer tasks or problems where I can grade the design or methods of others.
____   6. When making a decision, I like to compare the opposing points of view.
____   7. I like situations where I can compare and rate different ways of doing things.
____   8. I enjoy work that involves analyzing, grading, or comparing things.

Interpreting Scores

The way you evaluate your score is to add up the eight numbers you wrote down above, and then divide by 8. Carry out the division to one decimal place. You now should have a number between 1.0 and 7.0. There are six categories of scores, which depend on your status and your sex. These six categories are shown below.

Nonstudent Adults

	Category	Male	Female
Very High	(Top 1%–10%)	5.6–7.0	5.8–7.0
High	(Top 11%–25%)	5.3–5.5	5.2–5.7
High Middle	(Top 26%–50%)	4.6–5.2	4.8–5.1
Low Middle	(Top 51%–75%)	4.1–4.5	4.1–4.7
Low	(Top 76%–90%)	3.6–4.0	3.4–4.0
Very Low	(Top 91%–100%)	1.0–3.5	1.0–3.3

College Student Adults

	Category	Male	Female
Very High	(Top 1%–10%)	5.3–7.0	5.6–7.0
High	(Top 11%–25%)	4.6–5.2	5.0–5.5
High Middle	(Top 26%–50%)	4.2–4.5	4.6–4.9
Low Middle	(Top 51%–75%)	3.9–4.1	4.2–4.5
Low	(Top 76%–90%)	3.5–3.8	3.2–4.1
Very Low	(Top 91%–100%)	1.0–3.4	1.0–3.1

If you scored in the "very high" category, then you have all or almost all of the characteristics of a judicial person. If you scored in the "high" category, you have many of these characteristics. And if you scored in the "high middle" category, then you have at least some of the characteristics. If you scored in the bottom three categories, however, then this is not one of your preferred styles. Keep in mind, though, that just how judicial you are may vary across tasks, situations, and your time of life.

People with a judicial style are like Corwin in the vignette of the three college roommates in Chapter 1. They like to evaluate rules and procedures and to judge things. As reporters, for example, they would rather be columnists than straight news reporters, a job that requires a more executive type of thinking. As teachers, they may actually enjoy evaluating their students more than they enjoy teaching them. As supervisors, they may like rating their employees more than they like supervising them.

Judicial people also prefer problems in which they can analyze and evaluate things and ideas. For example, I am a primarily legislative person who has held a highly judicial role: editor of a journal (*Psychological Bulletin*). A journal editor's primary job is to evaluate the suitability of manuscripts for publication, a judicial job if ever there was one. But unlike many of my fellow editors, I feel uncomfortable evaluating manuscripts. So I tried to make a major part of my job one of innovation – redefining the priorities of the journal and dreaming up symposia that I thought would be exciting to readers. Again, jobs can be redefined, within limits, to accommodate the styles people have, just so long as the people make sure they get done what needs to get done.

Legislative and judicial people can work well together in a team. For example, selection procedures tend to be largely judicial, and are well suited to people who like to evaluate. I'm not so great on admissions and hiring committees, because I have trouble finding interest in reading and evaluating one candidate after another. I keep wondering who am I to judge, a doubt less likely to plague a judicial person. But where I have contributed to the admissions and hiring procedures, at least in my own department, is in trying to redefine the criteria that are used for admissions, for example, devising admissions procedures that place less emphasis on standardized-test scores and hiring procedures that place less emphasis on so-called objective measures (e.g., number of published articles) that may emphasize quantity rather than quality. The legislative person like myself may well not be ideal to read the applications and judge them, for lack of interest in doing the job the way it should be done; but the legislative person can work with the judicial person, suggesting some of the criteria the judicial person might use in making his or her evaluations.

Judicial people like to judge both structure and content. Thus, in the personal example above, they are as likely to judge the procedures I suggest for hiring people as they are the candidates to be hired. They thus serve a valuable function in making sure that the proposals of the more legislative people are, in fact, suitable ones. In my view, it is important that judicial people be given the training they need in order to judge things properly. For example, in education, there is no lack of judicial persons, but many such people are not trained in issues of experimental design and statistics, and so they are unable to conduct rigorous tests of educational reforms or other procedures that the schools implement. So they may end up making their judgments on the basis of information that is not as adequate as it ideally could or should be.

Some of the kinds of activities that judicial people prefer are writing critiques, giving opinions, judging people and their work, and evaluating programs. A literary critic, for example, is likely to be primarily judicial, whereas the writer whose work is being criticized is more likely to be legislative.

Some examples of occupations that tend to be particularly suitable for judicial people are judge, critic, program evaluator, admissions officer, grant or contract monitor, systems analyst, and consultant. Some of their special likes and dislikes are shown in Table 2.2.

Every organization needs judicial people as well as legislative and executive ones. Someone or some group has to formulate norms and plans; other people have to implement them; and other people have to make sure they are working. None of these styles is "better" than the others, simply because no organization could work over the long term without all of the styles being represented. An organization without legislative people would end up copying other organizations, and thereby always be running behind. An organization without executive people might have lots of plans that never would come to be implemented. And an organization without judicial people would be unsuccessful at evaluating which of its policies and plans were working and which were not.

Of course, these functions do not have to be fulfilled by separate people. The same person can and typically will perform all three of these functions in greater or lesser degree. But people often feel more comfortable in one role or another, and matching people to roles often facilitates the quality of the output in the organization, as well as leaving people happier with their responsibilities. It is therefore important to make sure that the functions are all represented in some way, and preferably in a way that leaves people happy with the responsibilities they are taking.

Table 2.2. *Likes and Dislikes of Judicial-Evaluators*

Likes	Dislikes
In School	
Comparing and contrasting literary characters	Remembering which literary characters did what, when
Analyzing the plot or themes of a story	Writing a story from scratch
Evaluating what is right and wrong with a scientific theory or experiment	Formulating a scientific theory or experiment
Correcting other people's work	Receiving an evaluation from a teacher with no reasons given for the evaluation.
Analyzing the reasons that a war started	Memorizing dates of wars
Evaluating the strategy of a competing sport team	Following a coach's directions without understanding why they were given
Analyzing the meaning of a work of fine art	Creating an original work of art
Finding what's wrong with a mathematical proof	Memorizing a mathematical proof
At Work	
Evaluating a business plan	Being presented with a business plan to be implemented
Judging the quality of a subordinate's work	Being assigned to help weaker subordinates
Analyzing the strengths and weaknesses of an advertising campaign	Creating an advertising campaign
Deciding how funds should be rationally allocated	Being told how funds will be allocated in your unit
Interviewing job candidates	Being forced to hire a designated job candidate
Comparing two contract proposals for their value to the company	Writing a contract proposal
Deciding how a subordinate's memorandum should be revised	Writing a memorandum that expresses someone else's evaluation of a situation

MEASUREMENT ISSUES

When we measure styles, we do not limit ourselves to the Sternberg-Wagner inventory, but rather try as well to devise assessments that take into account people's likes and dislikes in particular situations. In this way, we get a better sense of a person's styles in particular kinds of tasks and situations. For example, here are a couple of items assessing legislative, executive, and judicial styles in an academic context that Elena Grigorenko and I have given to students in our research:

1. When I am studying literature, I prefer:
   a. to make up my own story with my own characters and my own plot.
   b. to evaluate the author's style, to criticize the author's ideas, and to evaluate characters' actions.
   c. to follow a teacher's advice and interpretations of the author's ideas, to use a teacher's way of analyzing literature.
   d. to do something else (please describe your preference in the space below).
2. When I am studying history, I:
   a. try to understand and evaluate actions of historical figures.
   b. imagine how I would act under the same historical circumstances.
   c. understand that I have to learn a certain amount of information, even if I am not interested in the topic.
   d. do something else (please describe your preference in the space below).

These items give students an opportunity to select a legislative (1-a, 2-b), judicial (1-b, 2-a), or executive (1-c, 2-c) response. There is no right or wrong response, however. But note that the way a teacher teaches literature or history and then evaluates students is likely to end up favoring one style or another. The teacher who encourages students to express themselves creatively is likely to favor legislative students; the teacher who stresses critical analysis, interpretation, and comparison, to favor judicial students; and the teacher who stresses acceptance of his or her viewpoint as well as learning of "facts," to favor executive students.

Here are two more items, contrasting the executive style (3-a, 4-b) with the legislative one (3-b, 4-a):

3. After school I usually
   a. participate in a number of school-related clubs, organizations, or sports teams.
   b. go my own way; I do not like organized activities.
4. When I am shopping for new clothes I prefer to buy things that
   a. are different from anything anyone else is wearing so I can create my own style;
   b. are similar to things that my closest friends are wearing.

These items show just how domain-specific styles can be. Any number of people who might be legislative in school might be executive in their choice of clothing, or vice versa. We thus need to understand styles in the contexts in which they are expressed, including the styles considered in the next chapter, those that deal with the form of mental self-government.

3
Forms of Thinking Styles
The Monarchic, Hierarchic, Oligarchic, and Anarchic Styles

Ellen was a natural reader, but her brother, Craig, wasn't. As a concerned parent, of course, Craig's father wanted him to read. But his initial forays into trying to get his son to read were not very successful. The father had loved comic books as a child, and comic books had taught him a lot more about reading than did Dick, Jane, and Sally. No sale: Craig just wasn't interested. Then the father tried the Hardy boys – he'd read every one as a child. No sale: Craig found them boring. The father learned, as does every father, that what interests the father doesn't necessarily interest the son.

Craig has a tendency to be single-minded, and at the time he was single-minded about sports. His preoccupation with sports gave Craig's father an idea. He got Craig sports novels to read – stories about young boys who, like himself, were excited about sports, and whose life adventures revolved around sports. When the father was Craig's age, he had wanted to be a detective like the Hardy boys, but Craig wanted to be an athlete. Bingo: Craig started reading.

The father was able to get Craig to do what the father wanted and thought was right for him by capitalizing on one aspect of his styles of thinking. Craig tends to be monarchic, or single-minded.

Styles of government come in different forms, and so do the styles of people's mental self-government. Four of these forms are the monarchic, the hierarchic, the oligarchic, and the anarchic. By understanding your own and other people's forms of thinking, you will see better how to know yourself, and to know how to be effective with others.

44

THE MONARCHIC STYLE

Before reading on, you may wish to test and evaluate yourself on a scale measuring the monarchic style. If so, take Self-assessment 3.1.

Self-assessment 3.1. *Sternberg-Wagner Self-Assessment Inventory on the Monarchic Style*

Read each of the following statements, and then rate yourself on a 1–7 scale, where each rating corresponds to how well a statement describes you: 1 = Not at all well; 2 = Not very well; 3 = Slightly well; 4 = Somewhat well; 5 = Well; 6 = Very well; and 7 = Extremely well.

___ 1. When talking or writing about ideas, I stick to one main idea.

___ 2. I like to deal with major issues or themes, rather than details or facts.

___ 3. When trying to finish a task, I tend to ignore problems that come up.

___ 4. I use any means to reach my goal.

___ 5. When trying to make a decision, I tend to see only one major factor.

___ 6. If there are several important things to do, I do the one most important to me.

___ 7. I like to concentrate on one task at a time.

___ 8. I have to finish one project before starting another one.

Interpreting Scores

The way you evaluate your score is to add up the eight numbers you wrote down above, and then divide by 8. Carry out the division to one decimal place. You now should have a number between 1.0 and 7.0. There are six categories of scores, which depend on your status and your sex. These six categories are shown below.

	Nonstudent Adults		
	Category	Male	Female
Very High	(Top 1%–10%)	5.2–7.0	5.0–7.0
High	(Top 11%–25%)	4.6–5.1	4.1–4.9
High Middle	(Top 26%–50%)	4.1–4.5	3.8–4.0
Low Middle	(Top 51%–75%)	3.4–4.0	3.2–3.7
Low	(Top 76%–90%)	3.1–3.3	2.6–3.1
Very Low	(Top 91%–100%)	1.0–3.0	1.0–2.5

	College Student Adults		
	Category	Male	Female
Very High	(Top 1%–10%)	4.6–7.0	5.0–7.0
High	(Top 11%–25%)	4.1–4.5	4.4–4.9
High Middle	(Top 26%–50%)	3.6–4.0	4.0–4.3
Low Middle	(Top 51%–75%)	3.2–3.5	3.5–3.9
Low	(Top 76%–90%)	3.0–3.1	3.1–3.4
Very Low	(Top 91%–100%)	1.0–2.9	1.0–3.0

If you scored in the "very high" category, then you have all or almost all of the characteristics of a monarchic person. If you scored in the "high" category, you have many of these characteristics. And if you scored in the "high middle" category, then you have at least some of the characteristics. If you scored in the bottom three categories, then this is not one of your preferred styles. Keep in mind, though, that just how monarchic you are may vary across tasks, situations, and your time of life.

People who exhibit a predominantly monarchic style, like Craig, tend to be motivated by a single goal or need at a time. If you get married to one of these people, it usually doesn't take you long to find out. If the person is monarchic about something, or worse, someone, other than you, you're likely to find out rather quickly. The person who is monarchic about his or her work, for example, may not be around much! It can be worse when the spouse is monarchic about someone else, as in the case of Prince Charles of Great Britain, with his apparent obsession for Camilla Parker-Bowles. Of course, the fictional Scarlett O'Hara had the same monarchic obsession, toward Ashley rather than

Rhett. Unlike Prince Charles, however, she was unlikely ever truly to be a monarch!

Monarchic people also tend to be single-minded and driven by whatever they are single-minded about. Many people whom we fliply call "obsessive-compulsive" are not obsessive-compulsive in the strict clinical sense. A truly obsessive person, for example, has an all-consuming thought that cannot be put out of mind, however one tries. A truly compulsive person performs an action frequently that he or she would much rather not perform, such as continual hand-washing. A person who loves a coin collection or is consumed with the study of fine wines is typically not clinically obsessed. Stories about obsession are often really about people with a monarchic style.

Here's obsession, as depicted by Edgar Allan Poe:

It is impossible to say how first the idea entered my brain; but once conceived, it haunted me day and night. Object there was none. Passion there was none. I loved the old man. He had never wronged me. He had never given me insult. For his gold I had no desire. I think it was his eye! Yes, it was this! He had the eye of a vulture – a pale blue eye, with a film over it. Whenever it fell upon me, my blood ran cold; and so by degrees – very gradually – I made up my mind to take the life of the old man, and thus rid myself of the eye forever.[1]

Now here's an example from the same author of someone who's become rather monarchic, but not obsessed:

> But my heart it is brighter
>   Than all of the many
> Stars of the sky,
>   For it sparkles with Annie –
> It glows with the light
>   Of the love of my Annie –
> With the thought of the light
>   Of the eyes of my Annie.[2]

In "The Tell-Tale Heart," the protagonist cannot stop thinking about the eye, try as he might. In "For Annie," the protagonist chooses to think about the love he has lost to death, Annie.

Monarchic people have a tendency to see things in terms of their "issue." Richard Nixon, as president, became rather monarchic with respect to how his enemies were doing him in. Much of his administration came to be devoted to following these real and imagined enemies, and giving them their "due." This unfortunate direction of his energy was part of what led to Nixon's resignation as president.

The intense competition among businesses today, combined with downsizing, is probably an environmental factor that is contributing to managers being monarchic with respect to short-term bottom-line profit. The result is that workers can become so consumed with the need for short-term profits that long-term issues are put on the back burner or never dealt with at all.

Monarchic people often attempt to solve problems, full speed ahead, damn the obstacles. They can be decisive, and occasionally too decisive. For example, Jacques Chrétien, prime minister of Canada, was insufficiently attentive to the problem of Québec, and in a referendum in 1995, Québec came extremely close to voting to secede from Canada. Chrétien then belatedly became consumed by the Québec problem. He wanted to solve it, and solve it fast. He came up with a plan to divided Canada into four regions, the East, the West, Ontario, and Québec. This plan was perceived by some as lacking sensitivity, because it lumped together large numbers of provinces in both the eastern and western regions of Canada, giving Ontario and Québec priority. Moreover, the regions did not even reflect the relative proportions of population in Canada. For example, the western region had considerably more population than the eastern region. In becoming monarchic about solving a problem, one can lose sight of other people's priorities, as Chrétien appeared to do in this instance.

If a monarchic person cannot see how something relates to a preferred issue, the person may find the thing lacking in interest. This means that their interest can often be grabbed if one relates what one has to offer to their issue. Thus, political candidates quickly learn to tailor their speeches to their audiences, trying to hit on the hot-button issue or issues that are of concern to particular constituencies.

In education, teachers can often better reach children if they understand what they're monarchic about. Several years ago, when Craig was a student in middle school, he was getting B's in science, despite his keen interest in the subject. His mother went in to speak with his science teacher. By now, Craig's monarchic interest had switched from sports to computers. It is a characteristic of monarchic people that their interest may switch, but their tendency to be monarchic about something usually doesn't. Craig's mother asked the teacher if he was aware of Craig's strong interest in computers. He was. The mother suggested that if the teacher were somehow able to bring computer issues into the science classroom, Craig's interest, as well as that of other students, might be provoked. To his credit, the teacher did as Craig's mother suggested. Craig went from being a B-student to being an A-student, and perhaps other students did as well. Bring in the interest, and the performance can change quite quickly. But how about people who are not monarchic?

THE HIERARCHIC STYLE

Test yourself on the hierarchic style (Self-assessment 3.2) before reading on.

Self-assessment 3.2. *Sternberg-Wagner Self-Assessment Inventory on the Hierarchic Style*

Read each of the following statements, and then rate yourself on a 1–7 scale, where each rating corresponds to how well a statement describes you: 1 = Not at all well; 2 = Not very well; 3 = Slightly well; 4 = Somewhat well; 5 = Well; 6 = Very well; and 7 = Extremely well.

___ 1. I like to set priorities for the things I need to do before I start doing them.

___ 2. In talking or writing down ideas, I like to have the issues organized in order of importance.

___ 3. Before starting a project, I like to know the things I have to do and in what order.

___ 4. In dealing with difficulties, I have a good sense of how important each of them is and what order to tackle them in.

___ 5. When there are many things to do, I have a clear sense of the order in which to do them.

___ 6. When starting something, I like to make a list of things to do and to order the things by importance.

___ 7. When working on a task, I can see how the parts relate to the overall goal of the task.

___   8. When discussing or writing down ideas I stress the
main idea and how everything fits together.

Interpreting Scores

The way you evaluate your score is to add up the eight numbers
you wrote down above, and then divide by 8. Carry out the
division to one decimal place. You now should have a number
between 1.0 and 7.0. There are six categories of scores, which
depend on your status and your sex. These six categories are
shown below.

	Nonstudent Adults		
	Category	Male	Female
Very High	(Top 1%–10%)	6.2–7.0	6.5–7.0
High	(Top 11%–25%)	5.8–6.1	6.0–6.4
High Middle	(Top 26%–50%)	5.1–5.7	5.3–5.9
Low Middle	(Top 51%–75%)	4.5–5.0	4.2–5.2
Low	(Top 76%–90%)	4.1–4.4	3.4–4.1
Very Low	(Top 91%–100%)	1.0–4.0	1.0–3.3

	College Student Adults		
	Category	Male	Female
Very High	(Top 1%–10%)	6.8–7.0	6.1–7.0
High	(Top 11%–25%)	5.9–6.7	5.5–6.0
High Middle	(Top 26%–50%)	5.0–5.8	5.0–5.4
Low Middle	(Top 51%–75%)	4.8–4.9	4.3–4.9
Low	(Top 76%–90%)	4.0–4.7	3.9–4.2
Very Low	(Top 91%–100%)	1.0–3.9	1.0–3.8

If you scored in the "very high" category, then you have all or
almost all of the characteristics of a hierarchic person. If you
scored in the "high" category, you have many of these characteristics. And if you scored in the "high middle" category, then
you have at least some of the characteristics. If you scored in the
bottom three categories, then this is not one of your preferred
styles. Keep in mind, though, that just how hierarchic you are
may vary across tasks, situations, and your time of life.

People with a hierarchic style tend to be motivated by a hierarchy of goals, with the recognition that not all of the goals can be fulfilled equally well and that some goals are more important than others. They thus tend to be priority setters who allocate their resources carefully. Whereas monarchic people prefer to concentrate heavily on one thing – essentially to put all their eggs in one basket – hierarchic people like to divide up their resources.

I once had a student who, whenever she would come to meet with me in my office, would have a list of things she wanted to discuss. The list was always set up in order of priorities, so that she would first discuss the most important things, down to the least important things, which came last. In this way, if we didn't find time to talk about everything, she would have guaranteed for herself that the most important things, at least, were discussed. One day this student came into my office with what appeared to be a different kind of list. I expressed my awareness of her having changed the format of her list. I didn't get it quite right. She explained that what had happened was that she had come to have so many lists that now she had formed a list of lists. What I was looking at was this higher-order, master list. That's being hierarchical.

Hierarchic people tend to be systematic and organized in their solutions to problems and in their decision making. Perhaps this organization is part of what puts them at a great advantage in school and in many other institutions. Most institutions place hierarchic people at an advantage, and schools are perhaps the most notable. Students study multiple subjects, so they have to set priorities for their time and their expenditures of effort. They take tests that often are rather long for the time period, so that the hierarchic students will be at an advantage as they devise a system of priorities for finishing as much of the test as possible within the time period allotted. They tend to write in the hierarchic style preferred by teachers, and read in a way that distinguishes between more and less important points.

Is it ever bad to be hierarchic? It can be. Keep in mind that styles are not in and of themselves good or bad. For example, if one has a monumental project to get done, such as a doctoral dissertation, it may be more advantageous to be monarchic. Or if a company has a single goal, such as bottom-line profit, the monarchic person may be at an advantage in the realization of this goal. Hierarchic people can also become so fixated on the various elements of the hierarchy that they become indecisive. One needs to spend the time arranging the priorities, but also ensuring that they are carried out.

THE OLIGARCHIC STYLE

Test yourself on the oligarchic style (Self-assessment 3.3) before reading on.

Self-assessment 3.3. *Sternberg-Wagner Self-Assessment Inventory on the Oligarchic Style*

Read each of the following statements, and then rate yourself on a 1–7 scale, where each rating corresponds to how well a statement describes you: 1 = Not at all well; 2 = Not very well; 3 = Slightly well; 4 = Somewhat well; 5 = Well; 6 = Very well; and 7 = Extremely well.

— 1. When I undertake some task, I am usually equally open to starting by working on any of several things.

— 2. When there are competing issues of importance to address in my work, I somehow try to address them simultaneously.

— 3. Usually when I have many things to do, I split my time and attention equally among them.

— 4. I try to have several things going on at once, so that I can shift back and forth between them.

— 5. Usually I do several things at once.

— 6. I sometimes have trouble setting priorities for multiple things that I need to get done.

— 7. I usually know what things need to be done, but I sometimes have trouble deciding in what order to do them.

— 8. Usually when working on a project, I tend to view almost all aspects of it as equally important.

Interpreting Scores

The way you evaluate your score is to add up the eight numbers you wrote down above, and then divide by 8. Carry out the division to one decimal place. You now should have a number between 1.0 and 7.0. There are six categories of scores, which depend on your status and your sex. These six categories are shown below.

	Nonstudent Adults		
	Category	Male	Female
Very High	(Top 1%–10%)	5.3–7.0	5.3–7.0
High	(Top 11%–25%)	4.7–5.2	4.5–5.2
High Middle	(Top 26%–50%)	3.7–4.6	3.5–4.4
Low Middle	(Top 51%–75%)	2.6–3.6	2.8–3.4
Low	(Top 76%–90%)	1.9–2.5	2.1–2.7
Very Low	(Top 91%–100%)	1.0–1.8	1.0–2.0

	College Student Adult		
	Category	Male	Female
Very High	(Top 1%–10%)	4.4–7.0	5.0–7.0
High	(Top 11%–25%)	4.0–4.3	4.3–4.9
High Middle	(Top 26%–50%)	3.4–3.9	3.8–4.2
Low Middle	(Top 51%–75%)	2.8–3.3	3.0–3.7
Low	(Top 76%–90%)	2.1–2.7	2.4–2.9
Very Low	(Top 91%–100%)	1.0–2.0	1.0–2.3

If you scored in the "very high" category, then you have all or almost all of the characteristics of an oligarchic person. If you scored in the "high" category, you have many of these characteristics. And if you scored in the "high middle" category, then you have at least some of the characteristics. If you scored in the bottom three categories, then this is not one of your preferred styles. Keep in mind, though, that just how oligarchic you are may vary across tasks, situations, and your time of life.

In an oligarchy, several individuals share power equally. Individuals with the oligarchic style tend to be motivated by several, often competing goals of equal perceived importance. They have trouble deciding which goals to give priority to. The result is that they may have trouble allocating resources. They may have the ability to do excellent work, but it doesn't always show through if they are in a situation that requires resource allocation.

Some years back, I had a secretary who did competent work, but who always seemed to be doing first what I needed done last. If I gave her three or four things to do, the one thing I could be sure of was that the one I didn't need for a while would get done first, and the one that was urgent would get done last. I eventually reached the point where I couldn't tolerate the frustration I was experiencing, and decided I needed either to find another secretary, or to make things work in a very different way with her.

I then had what at the time seemed like a brainstorm, but in retrospect seems quite obvious. I started a new procedure whereby every time I gave her work, I rated its priority on a 1 (first priority) to 3 (last priority) scale. Thus, rather than leaving it to her intuition to understand what I needed quickly, I told her directly. Her work immediately changed completely, and she stayed with me as an effective worker for many years more.

Because oligarchic people do not take to it naturally, they may need to be guided in the setting of priorities. In instances where there is sufficient time or there are sufficient resources to get everything done, their oligarchic style may not even show through. But in instances where there is a resource allocation problem, either direct guidance or other forms of assistance can make them potentially quite effective.

In a way, an oligarchic person is a cross between a monarchic person and a hierarchic one. Like the monarchic person, the oligarchic one is not a natural priority setter. And like the hierarchic person, the oligarchic person likes to do multiple things at once. In fact, in situations where there are no resource limitations, the oligarchic person may be indistinguishable from the hierarchic one.

The oligarchic style might seem like a slightly worse version of the hierarchic style – perhaps a mutated version that has lost its sense of priorities. But arguably, there can be instances where the oligarchic style works as well or better. Think for a moment of a government, or a business organization. A hierarchy, once entrenched, can become rigid.

Sometimes organizations suffer because they acquire layer after layer of hierarchy – usually at the middle management level – eventually to the point where the layers stop serving a purpose. A less hierarchical organization often has more flexibility, and can change more quickly to adapt to changing circumstances. A less hierarchical person, similarly, may set up fewer roadblocks to flexible performance, and in some instances might actually perform better than the hierarchic one. At the same time, where a hierarchy of goals or priorities or whatever may be needed, the hierarchic person will be at an advantage.

Oligarchic employees and students sometimes suffer because they have competing demands on their time, and if, for example, they have short-term and long-term projects, they may find themselves putting their time into one set of projects and neglecting the other. People in managerial and other kinds of jobs sometimes fail because they pay attention to the pressing short-term issues, but fail to allow time for the less pressing, but ultimately perhaps more important, long-term issues. Sometimes, they lose out just because the competition was attending to the long term.

An example of how an oligarchic style can either facilitate or hinder one in life can be seen in the tradeoff between professional and personal time. A hierarchic person sets up a set of priorities and tries to follow them. The person is at an advantage in having priorities and sticking to them, but may be at a disadvantage if the priorities need to shift for, say, short periods of time; but the person doesn't realize this, and stays with the now nonoptimal priorities. The oligarchic person may be able more flexibly to switch priorities. But this person may be more likely to be buffeted by whatever is most pressing at the moment, costing a great deal in terms of what is being ignored.

Jack was pretty typical of graduates from prestigious law schools who go to work as associates for high-powered law firms. During the initial few years, he was expected to devote an enormous amount of time – 80 hours per week was not unusual – to the firm. He figured that he would devote the energy he needed to devote to the law in the early years, and would later have time for his wife, once he had become a partner and the pressure had eased. It wasn't any kind of a principled decision – it was simply that the law firm was putting on the pressure, and his wife wasn't.

Eventually, Jack's wife tried in various ways to tell him that he needed to think about the marriage too, but Jack was always just about ready to do so. Ultimately, his work went well, but as so often happens, his marriage didn't, and by the time he made partner, he didn't have to worry about devoting more time to his wife, because he no longer had one. Had Jack self-consciously and purposely decided that the work was worth more than the marriage, perhaps the failure of the marriage would have been an acceptable cost. Jack never made such a decision, however. He just drifted into a pattern, as people so easily can do, and later paid for it.

THE ANARCHIC STYLE

Before reading about the anarchic style, take Self-assessment 3.4 and then score yourself.

Self-assessment 3.4. *Sternberg-Wagner Self-Assessment Inventory on the Anarchic Style*

Read each of the following statements, and then rate yourself on a 1–7 scale, where each rating corresponds to how well a statement describes you: 1 = Not at all well; 2 = Not very well; 3 = Slightly well; 4 = Somewhat well; 5 = Well; 6 = Very well; and 7 = Extremely well.

____ 1. When I have many things to do, I do whatever occurs to me first.

____ 2. I can switch from one task to another easily, because all tasks seem to me to be equally important.

____ 3. I like to tackle all kinds of problems, even seemingly trivial ones.

____ 4. When discussing or writing down ideas, I use whatever comes to mind.

____ 5. I find that solving one problem usually leads to many other ones, that are just as important.

____ 6. When trying to make a decision, I try to take all points of view into account.

____ 7. When there are many important things to do, I try to do as many as I can in whatever time I have.

___ 8. When I start on a task, I like to consider all possible ways of doing it, even the most ridiculous.

Interpreting Scores

The way you evaluate your score is to add up the eight numbers you wrote down above, and then divide by 8. Carry out the division to one decimal place. You now should have a number between 1.0 and 7.0. There are six categories of scores, which depend on your status and your sex. These six categories are shown below.

Nonstudent Adults

	Category	Male	Female
Very High	(Top 1%–10%)	5.8–7.0	5.8–7.0
High	(Top 11%–25%)	5.4–5.7	5.4–5.7
High Middle	(Top 26%–50%)	4.9–5.3	4.8–5.3
Low Middle	(Top 51%–75%)	4.1–4.8	4.0–4.7
Low	(Top 76%–90%)	3.5–4.0	3.5–3.9
Very Low	(Top 91%–100%)	1.0–3.4	1.0–3.4

College Student Adults

	Category	Male	Female
Very High	(Top 1%–10%)	5.2–7.0	5.5–7.0
High	(Top 11%–25%)	4.8–5.1	4.9–5.4
High Middle	(Top 26%–50%)	4.5–4.7	4.4–4.8
Low Middle	(Top 51%–75%)	3.9–4.4	3.8–4.3
Low	(Top 76%–90%)	3.4–3.8	3.4–3.7
Very Low	(Top 91%–100%)	1.0–3.3	1.0–3.3

If you scored in the "very high" category, then you have all or almost all of the characteristics of an anarchic person. If you scored in the "high" category, you have many of these characteristics. And if you scored in the "high middle" category, then you have at least some of the characteristics. If you scored in the bottom three categories, then this is not one of your preferred styles. Keep in mind, though, that just how anarchic you are may vary across tasks, situations, and your time of life.

People with an anarchic style tend to be motivated by a wide assortment of needs and goals that are often difficult for others, as well as for themselves, to sort out. They tend to be not so much asystematic as antisystematic. They are likely to disdain the system in place, sometimes with good reason, but other times for less clear reasons. As a result, they tend to be unwelcome in most organizational settings.

In schools, anarchic students are at risk for antisocial behavior. They don't fit in, so they drop out, whether physically or psychologically. Even when they are part of the school, they stick out like sore thumbs. They are the students who challenge teachers, not necessarily on principled grounds, but rather for the sake of challenging the teachers or any other authority figures. But as authority figures themselves, they tend to be unsuccessful, because they are no better at maintaining their own systems than at adhering to anyone else's.

Anarchic people further tend to take a random approach to problems. When placed in a conversation with hierarchical people, the two kinds of people can drive each other nuts. The anarchic person tends to be "all over the place" and to have trouble following any straight line of conversation. The hierarchic person, on the other hand, expects at least a semblance of order. Anarchic people tend to be simplifiers at times, and to have trouble setting priorities because they have no firm set of rules upon which to base these priorities.

The anarchic style would seem to be unlike other styles in being a "bad" style – after all, who in an institution wants anarchists around? Is this style an exception to the generalization that styles are not good or bad, but rather differentially useful in different situations? I believe not. Anarchic people have several important contributions they can make. Not the least of these is to challenge the system, if people can retain their patience with the anarchist.

Equally important, anarchic people often have a certain potential for creativity that is rare in others. Why? Because anarchists are willing to grab a little from here, a little from there, and a little from somewhere else. They are not constrained by the boundaries that people normally throw up between domains of thought and action. They are willing to reach out and bring things together in ways that most people would never consider. As a teacher, I see it as my role to try to help anarchic people gain sufficient self-organization and self-discipline that they can master their creative impulses, rather than letting them diffuse in the wind. Anarchic people can have a lot to offer if they are able to channel their offerings effectively. So they, like anyone else, have a contribution to make in a complex and ever-changing society.

4

Levels, Scope, and Leanings of Thinking Styles

The Global, Local, Internal, External, Liberal, and Conservative Styles

Thinking styles can differ in level, scope, and leaning. Let's see what each of these means.

LEVELS OF THINKING STYLES: GLOBAL AND LOCAL STYLES

Before reading about the global and local styles, take Self-assessments 4.1 and 4.2, and then score them.

Self-assessment 4.1. *Sternberg-Wagner Self-Assessment Inventory on the Global Style*

Read each of the following statements, and then rate yourself on a 1–7 scale, where each rating corresponds to how well a statement describes you: 1 = Not at all well; 2 = Not very well; 3 = Slightly well; 4 = Somewhat well; 5 = Well; 6 = Very well; and 7 = Extremely well.

____ 1. I like situations or tasks in which I am not concerned with details.

____ 2. I care more about the general effect than about the details of a task I have to do.

____ 3. In doing a task, I like to see how what I do fits into the general picture.

____ 4. I tend to emphasize the general aspect of issues or the overall effect of a project.

___ 5. I like situations where I can focus on general issues, rather than on specifics.

___ 6. In talking or writing down ideas, I like to show the scope and context of my ideas, that is, the general picture.

___ 7. I tend to pay little attention to details.

___ 8. I like working on projects that deal with general issues and not with nitty-gritty details.

Interpreting Scores

The way you evaluate your score is to add up the eight numbers you wrote down above, and then divide by 8. Carry out the division to one decimal place. You now should have a number between 1.0 and 7.0. There are six categories of scores, which depend on your status and your sex. These six categories are shown below.

Nonstudent Adults

	Category	Male	Female
Very High	(Top 1%–10%)	5.5–7.0	5.2–7.0
High	(Top 11%–25%)	4.9–5.4	4.8–5.1
High Middle	(Top 26%–50%)	4.4–4.8	4.0–4.7
Low Middle	(Top 51%–75%)	3.6–4.3	3.5–3.9
Low	(Top 76%–90%)	3.2–3.5	3.1–3.4
Very Low	(Top 91%–100%)	1.0–3.1	1.0–3.0

College Student Adults

	Category	Male	Female
Very High	(Top 1%–10%)	5.3–7.0	5.5–7.0
High	(Top 11%–25%)	4.5–5.2	4.8–5.4
High Middle	(Top 26%–50%)	4.0–4.4	4.1–4.7
Low Middle	(Top 51%–75%)	3.5–3.9	3.6–4.0
Low	(Top 76%–90%)	3.1–3.4	2.9–3.5
Very Low	(Top 91%–100%)	1.0–3.0	1.0–2.8

If you scored in the "very high" category, then you have all or almost all of the characteristics of the global person. If you scored in the "high" category, you have many of these characteristics. And if you scored in the "high middle" category, then you have at least some of the characteristics. If you scored in the bottom three categories, then this is not one of your preferred styles. Keep in mind, though, that just how global you are may vary across tasks, situations, and your time of life.

Self-assessment 4.2. *Sternberg-Wagner Self-Assessment Inventory on the Local Style*

Read each of the following statements, and then rate yourself on a 1–7 scale, where each rating corresponds to how well a statement describes you: 1 = Not at all well; 2 = Not very well; 3 = Slightly well; 4 = Somewhat well; 5 = Well; 6 = Very well; and 7 = Extremely well.

—   1. I prefer to deal with specific problems rather than with general questions.
—   2. I prefer tasks dealing with a single, concrete problem, rather than general or multiple ones.
—   3. I tend to break down a problem into many smaller ones that I can solve, without looking at the problem as a whole.
—   4. I like to collect detailed or specific information for projects I work on.
—   5. I like problems where I need to pay attention to detail.
—   6. I pay more attention to the parts of a task than to its overall effect or significance.
—   7. In discussing or writing on a topic, I think the details and facts are more important than the overall picture.
—   8. I like to memorize facts and bits of information without any particular content.

Interpreting Scores

The way you evaluate your score is to add up the eight numbers you wrote down above, and then divide by 8. Carry out the division to one decimal place. You now should have a number between 1.0 and 7.0. There are six categories of scores, which depend on your status and your sex. These six categories are shown below.

Nonstudent Adults

	Category	Male	Female
Very High	(Top 1%–10%)	5.1–7.0	5.1–7.0
High	(Top 11%–25%)	4.4–5.0	4.4–5.0
High Middle	(Top 26%–50%)	3.9–4.3	3.8–4.3
Low Middle	(Top 51%–75%)	3.6–3.8	3.4–3.7
Low	(Top 76%–90%)	3.4–3.5	3.0–3.3
Very Low	(Top 91%–100%)	1.0–3.3	1.0–2.9

College Student Adults

	Category	Male	Female
Very High	(Top 1%–10%)	4.9–7.0	4.5–7.0
High	(Top 11%–25%)	4.4–4.8	4.3–4.4
High Middle	(Top 26%–50%)	3.8–4.3	4.0–4.2
Low Middle	(Top 51%–75%)	3.2–3.7	3.5–3.9
Low	(Top 76%–90%)	2.8–3.1	2.9–3.4
Very Low	(Top 91%–100%)	1.0–2.7	1.0–2.8

If you scored in the "very high" category, then you have all or almost all of the characteristics of the local person. If you scored in the "high" category, you have many of these characteristics. And if you scored in the "high middle" category, then you have at least some of the characteristics. If you scored in the bottom three categories, then this is not one of your preferred styles. Keep in mind, though, that just how local you are may vary across tasks, situations, and your time of life.

As a college professor, I supervise student research. I try to help students find a research project that will be interesting and meaningful to them. Several years ago, I had a senior come to me who was interested in doing research. I asked her what she was interested in. She said, "Child development." So I asked, "What particular aspects of child development?" She replied, "All of child development." "Is there anything about child development you find especially interesting?" I asked. "I find it all interesting," she replied. And so the conversation went. With a freshman, maybe, the exchange would have been understandable. But in a senior who had nearly completed a psychology major, it was surprising. She just refused to focus her interests at all.

Of course, I've had essentially the opposite experience as well. Several years ago I had a report turned back to me that I had submitted to a government agency. Along with the report was a brief explanatory note from someone I'd never heard of explaining that the margins were, as I recall, seven-eights of an inch wide, whereas governmental regulations required them to be one inch. Would I please resubmit the report with the correct margins? I did as I was told, but found myself wondering about who this unknown individual was who sat in a governmental cubbyhole somewhere, ruler in hand, measuring the margins of submitted documents.

These two individuals, the psychology major and the government bureaucrat, are extreme examples of the global and local styles, respectively. Local people prefer to deal with details, global people with the big picture. Just as governments function at multiple levels, for example, federal, state (or provincial), county, city, and so on, so do people. Although the global and local styles are often viewed as two ends of the same continuum, they are not necessarily expressed in that way. Most people tend to be either more global or more local: They focus either more on the big picture or more on the small details. But some people are both: They are equally attentive to the big picture and to the little details. Moreover, these people may be more attentive to both the global and the local picture than other people are to either. Other people may be either global or local, but show different stylistic tendencies in different domains. Thus, in our experience, although the two styles are usually contrasted with each other, they don't have to be.

Global people, then, prefer to deal with relatively larger and often abstract issues. They tend to focus on the forest, sometimes at the expense of the trees. Their constant challenge is to stay grounded and not to get lost on Cloud Nine. The student who was interested in child development was not able, even after a fairly long discussion, to pin down her potential interests enough for us to formulate any concrete hypotheses. She insisted on staying at the level of "child development," which is fine as an interest, but which in and of itself does not lead to testable hypotheses.

Local people prefer to deal with details, sometimes minute ones, and often ones surrounding concrete issues. They tend to focus on the trees, sometimes at the expense of the forest. Their constant challenge is to see the whole forest, and not just its individual elements. The government bureaucrat presumably has a local style, at least in his work. He somehow manages to rationalize to himself salary received for checking margins and who knows what else on documents submitted to a particular agency.

Although most people have a preference to work at either a more global or a more local level, a key to successful problem solving in many situations is being able to traverse between levels. If one is more interested in working at a given level, it is often helpful to pair up with someone more interested in the other level. As more of a globalist in my research, I like nothing better than to work with localists, who attend to the details I often miss. We often value most the people who are the most like ourselves, but in collaborations, we often stand to benefit most from people who are moderately unlike ourselves with respect to their preferred level of processing. Too much overlap leads to some levels of functioning simply being ignored. Two globalists, for example, may do well in forming ideas, but will need someone to take care of the details of conceptualizing or implementing them. Two localists may help each other in pinning things down, but may need someone to set down the global issues that need to be dealt with in the first place.

If two people are close to the extremes – an extreme globalist and an extreme localist – they may find it hard to work together, not because they don't need each other, but because they cannot communicate well. They may not be well able to see each other's issues.

In early stages of careers, where one is largely self-dependent, inability to switch between levels of processing may be disastrous. Later, when one may have subordinates, it may be possible to delegate tasks requiring levels of functioning different from one's own preferred one.

In my own career, I have over time taken more to delegating local-level tasks, which I generally do not enjoy. Earlier in my career, there would have been no one to whom I could have delegated these tasks, so I had to be able to work at these levels myself. In general, successively higher levels of responsibility demand successively more global functioning. Sometimes, people promoted for their success at more local levels of functioning may be stymied by their jobs as the tasks they confront become more and more global. Unfortunately, some of the globalists will already have been selected out because they could not comfortably handle the local tasks required earlier in their careers. But of course, promotion does not necessarily mean more global responsibilities: Researchers promoted into administration, for example, often find themselves confronting exactly the opposite challenge: how to go from running a lab to handling mind-boggling administrative details.

SCOPE OF THINKING STYLES: INTERNAL AND EXTERNAL STYLES

Before reading about the internal and external styles, take Self-assessments 4.3 and 4.4, and then score yourself.

Self-assessment 4.3. *Sternberg-Wagner Self-Assessment Inventory on the Internal Style*

Read each of the following statements, and then rate yourself on a 1–7 scale, where each rating corresponds to how well a statement describes you: 1 = Not at all well; 2 = Not very well; 3 = Slightly well; 4 = Somewhat well; 5 = Well; 6 = Very well; and 7 = Extremely well.

___ 1. I like to control all phases of a project, without having to consult others.

___ 2. When trying to make a decision, I rely on my own judgment of the situation.

___ 3. I prefer situations where I can carry out my own ideas, without relying on others.

___ 4. When discussing or writing down ideas, I only like to use my own ideas.

___ 5. I like projects that I can complete independently.

___ 6. I prefer to read reports for information I need, rather than ask others for it.

___ 7. When faced with a problem, I like to work it out by myself.

___   8. I like to work alone on a task or problem.

Interpreting Scores

The way you evaluate your score is to add up the eight numbers you wrote down above, and then divide by 8. Carry out the division to one decimal place. You now should have a number between 1.0 and 7.0. There are six categories of scores, which depend on your status and your sex. These six categories are shown below.

Nonstudent Adult

	Category	Male	Female
Very High	(Top 1%–10%)	6.1–7.0	6.1–7.0
High	(Top 11%–25%)	5.4–6.0	5.2–6.0
High Middle	(Top 26%–50%)	4.8–5.3	4.2–5.1
Low Middle	(Top 51%–75%)	3.8–4.7	3.3–4.1
Low	(Top 76%–90%)	3.4–3.7	2.5–3.2
Very Low	(Top 91%–100%)	1.0–3.3	1.0–2.4

College Student Adults

	Category	Male	Female
Very High	(Top 1%–10%)	5.3–7.0	5.0–7.0
High	(Top 11%–25%)	4.5–5.2	4.5–4.9
High Middle	(Top 26%–50%)	3.9–4.4	4.0–4.4
Low Middle	(Top 51%–75%)	3.1–3.8	3.5–3.9
Low	(Top 76%–90%)	2.8–3.0	3.0–3.4
Very Low	(Top 91%–100%)	1.0–2.7	1.0–2.9

If you scored in the "very high" category, then you have all or almost all of the characteristics of the internal person. If you scored in the "high" category, you have many of these characteristics. And if you scored in the "high middle" category, then you have at least some of the characteristics. If you scored in the bottom three categories, then this is not one of your preferred styles. Keep in mind, though, that just how internal you are may vary across tasks, situations, and your time of life.

Self-assessment 4.4. *Sternberg-Wagner Self-Assessment Inventory on the External Style*

Read each of the following statements, and then rate yourself on a 1–7 scale, where each rating corresponds to how well a statement describes you: 1 = Not at all well; 2 = Not very well; 3 = Slightly well; 4 = Somewhat well; 5 = Well; 6 = Very well; and 7 = Extremely well.

—— 1. When starting a task, I like to brainstorm ideas with friends or peers.
—— 2. If I need more information, I prefer to talk about it with others rather than to read reports on it.
—— 3. I like to participate in activities where I can interact with others as a part of a team.
—— 4. I like projects in which I can work together with others.
—— 5. I like situations where I interact with others and everyone works together.
—— 6. In a discussion or report, I like to combine my own ideas with those of others.
—— 7. When working on a project, I like to share ideas and get input from other people.
—— 8. When making a decision, I try to take the opinions of others into account.

Interpreting Scores

The way you evaluate your score is to add up the eight numbers you wrote down above, and then divide by 8. Carry out the division to one decimal place. You now should have a number between 1.0 and 7.0. There are six categories of scores, which depend on your status and your sex. These six categories are shown below.

	Nonstudent Adults	
Category	Male	Female
Very High	(Top 1%–10%)	6.1–7.0	6.1–7.0
High	(Top 11%–25%)	5.7–6.0	5.7–6.0

High Middle	(Top 26%–50%)	5.0–5.6	4.8–5.6
Low Middle	(Top 51%–75%)	4.0–4.9	4.1–4.7
Low	(Top 76%–90%)	3.2–3.9	3.0–4.0
Very Low	(Top 91%–100%)	1.0–3.1	1.0–2.9

College Student Adults

	Category	Male	Female
Very High	(Top 1%–10%)	6.2–7.0	6.0–7.0
High	(Top 11%–25%)	5.6–6.1	5.6–5.9
High Middle	(Top 26%–50%)	5.1–5.5	4.9–5.5
Low Middle	(Top 51%–75%)	4.1–5.0	4.0–4.8
Low	(Top 76%–90%)	3.8–4.0	2.8–3.9
Very Low	(Top 91%–100%)	1.0–3.7	1.0–2.7

If you scored in the "very high" category, then you have all or almost all of the characteristics of the external person. If you scored in the "high" category, you have many of these characteristics. And if you scored in the "high middle" category, then you have at least some of the characteristics. If you scored in the bottom three categories, then this is not one of your preferred styles. Keep in mind, though, that just how external you are may vary across tasks, situations, and your time of life.

Governments need to deal both with internal, or domestic, affairs, and with external, or foreign, ones. Similarly, mental self-governments need to deal with both internal and external issues, as people find out every day in their personal lives and at work.

Helen has sold more telecommunications systems than any of her fellow salespeople. Her record in selling systems seems phenomenal to those who are just starting out. These novices often think that Helen has some kind of edge – contacts or perhaps lists of particularly eager customers. In fact, she does have an edge, but it is nothing secret. Helen puts her relationship with her customers first, and the particular product she is selling second. In this way, she has in fact gained more contacts. Putting the relationship first means that she listens to what customers want before trying to sell them anything, and that sometimes she will sell a less expensive telecommunications system, or even won't sell one at all, when she can show the customer how better to exploit the system they have. To most salespeople, her strategies would seem counterproductive, because she actually loses commission dollars by selling cheaper systems, and loses sales by showing customers how to exploit existing services. What she gains is an unequaled record of repeat buyers who specifically ask for her. The customer loyalty pays off over the years, so that she is able to build a larger steady customer base than any of her competitors.

Ron is one of Helen's competitors. Ron knows telecommunications systems even better than Helen does, and is probably even more interested in them than Helen is. His ideal would be to design the software for such systems rather than to sell them, but he doesn't have the training in software design, so he does the best he can, given the training he has, and his goal is eventually to move into systems design. Despite his knowledge, Ron does not sell nearly as many systems as does Helen. The reason: He puts the system, not the customer, first. His interest in the system attracts some customers, but his lesser interest in interacting with customers turns others off.

People with an internal style tend to be introverted, task-oriented, sometimes aloof, and socially less sensitive than other people. At times, they also lack interpersonal awareness, if only because they do not focus on it. People with an external style, in contrast, tend to be more extroverted, people-oriented, outgoing, socially more sensitive, and interpersonally more aware.

Some people prefer to work alone and to deal on an individual basis with the worlds of things and ideas. Other people prefer to work with others and to deal with the world of people. Again, most people are not strictly one or the other style, but alternate somewhere between them as a function of task and situation. In both education and job placement, bright individuals who are forced to work in a style that does not suit them may perform below their actual capabilities.

In management, a distinction is sometimes made between task-oriented and people-oriented managers.[1] This distinction is roughly comparable to that between internalists and externalists. In schooling, we sometimes find students who prefer working individually, whereas other students prefer working in groups. Traditionally, our system of schooling has tended to benefit internalists with at least some minor external orientation. Indeed, in many settings in school, such as on most tests, group work is considered cheating. Today, with increasing emphasis on cooperative (group) learning, the pendulum has started shifting in the opposite direction. Educators seem unwilling to accept the fact that there is no one best method of instruction, but rather that students need a variety of methods of instruction, including both individual and group learning.

For all the emphasis on individual performance in many school settings, much of people's performance after schooling is over will be in groups. Unfortunately, many people have had little experience or instruction in how to work in groups. The imbalance can be unfortunate, because group performance may be hindered not by the individuals in the group, but by the low quality of their interaction.[2]

LEANINGS OF THINKING STYLES: LIBERAL AND CONSERVATIVE STYLES

Before reading on, take Self-assessments 4.5 and 4.6.

Self-assessment 4.5. *Sternberg-Wagner Self-Assessment Inventory on the Liberal Style*

Read each of the following statements, and then rate yourself on a 1–7 scale, where each rating corresponds to how well a statement describes you: 1 = Not at all well; 2 = Not very well; 3 = Slightly well; 4 = Somewhat well; 5 = Well; 6 = Very well; and 7 = Extremely well.

___ 1. I enjoy working on projects that allow me to try novel ways of doing things.

___ 2. I like situations where I can try new ways of doing things.

___ 3. I like to change routines in order to improve the way tasks are done.

___ 4. I like to challenge old ideas or ways of doing things and to seek better ones.

___ 5. When faced with a problem, I prefer to try new strategies or methods to solve it.

___ 6. I like projects that allow me to look at a situation from a new perspective.

—— 7. I like to find old problems and find new methods to solve them.

—— 8. I like to do things in new ways not used by others in the past.

Interpreting Scores

The way you evaluate your score is to add up the eight numbers you wrote down above, and then divide by 8. Carry out the division to one decimal place. You now should have a number between 1.0 and 7.0. There are six categories of scores, which depend on your status and your sex. These six categories are shown below.

	Nonstudent Adults		
	Category	Male	Female
Very High	(Top 1%–10%)	6.6–7.0	6.5–7.0
High	(Top 11%–25%)	6.0–6.5	6.1–6.4
High Middle	(Top 26%–50%)	5.5–5.9	5.4–6.0
Low Middle	(Top 51%–75%)	4.9–5.4	4.5–5.3
Low	(Top 76%–90%)	4.1–4.8	3.3–4.4
Very Low	(Top 91%–100%)	1.0–4.0	1.0–3.2

	College Student Adults		
	Category	Male	Female
Very High	(Top 1%–10%)	6.3–7.0	6.0–7.0
High	(Top 11%–25%)	5.6–6.2	5.8–5.9
High Middle	(Top 26%–50%)	5.0–5.5	5.0–5.7
Low Middle	(Top 51%–75%)	4.1–4.9	4.2–4.9
Low	(Top 76%–90%)	3.6–4.0	3.8–4.1
Very Low	(Top 91%–100%)	1.0–3.5	1.0–3.7

If you scored in the "very high" category, then you have all or almost all of the characteristics of the liberal person. If you scored in the "high" category, you have many of these characteristics. And if you scored in the "high middle" category, then you have at least some of the characteristics. If you scored in the bottom three categories, then this is not one of your preferred styles. Keep in mind, though, that just how liberal you are may vary across tasks, situations, and your time of life.

Self-assessment 4.6. *Sternberg-Wagner Self-Assessment Inventory on the Conservative Style*

Read each of the following statements, and then rate yourself on a 1–7 scale, where each rating corresponds to how well a statement describes you: 1 = Not at all well; 2 = Not very well; 3 = Slightly well; 4 = Somewhat well; 5 = Well; 6 = Very well; and 7 = Extremely well.

___ 1. I like to do things in ways that have been used in the past.
___ 2. When I'm in charge of something, I like to follow methods and ideas used in the past.
___ 3. I like tasks and problems that have fixed rules to follow in order to complete them.
___ 4. I dislike problems that arise when doing something in the usual, customary way.
___ 5. I stick to standard rules or ways of doing things.
___ 6. I like situations where I can follow a set routine.
___ 7. When faced with a problem, I like to solve it in a traditional way.
___ 8. I like situations where the role I play is a traditional one.

Interpreting Scores

The way you evaluate your score is to add up the eight numbers you wrote down above, and then divide by 8. Carry out the division to one decimal place. You now should have a number between 1.0 and 7.0. There are six categories of scores, which depend on your status and your sex. These six categories are shown below.

		Nonstudent Adults	
	Category	Male	Female
Very High	(Top 1%–10%)	5.4–7.0	5.1–7.0

High	(Top 11%–25%)	4.6–5.3	4.4–5.0
High Middle	(Top 26%–50%)	3.8–4.5	3.4–4.3
Low Middle	(Top 51%–75%)	3.1–3.7	2.9–3.3
Low	(Top 76%–90%)	2.2–3.0	2.2–2.8
Very Low	(Top 91%–100%)	1.0–2.1	1.0–2.1

College Student Adults

	Category	Male	Female
Very High	(Top 1%–10%)	4.8–7.0	4.8–7.0
High	(Top 11%–25%)	4.2–4.7	4.4–4.7
High Middle	(Top 26%–50%)	3.9–4.1	3.8–4.3
Low Middle	(Top 51%–75%)	3.1–3.8	3.2–3.7
Low	(Top 76%–90%)	2.4–3.0	2.8–3.1
Very Low	(Top 91%–100%)	1.0–2.3	1.0–2.7

If you scored in the "very high" category, then you have all or almost all of the characteristics of the conservative person. If you scored in the "high" category, you have many of these characteristics. And if you scored in the "high middle" category, then you have at least some of the characteristics. If you scored in the bottom three categories, then this is not one of your preferred styles. Keep in mind, though, that just how conservative you are may vary across tasks, situations, and your time of life.

Individuals with a liberal style like to go beyond existing rules and procedures and seek to maximize change. They also seek or are at least comfortable with ambiguous situations, and prefer some degree of unfamiliarity in life and work. Individuals with a conservative style like to adhere to existing rules and procedures, minimize change, avoid ambiguous situations where possible, and prefer familiarity in life and work.

We are most familiar and often comfortable with people whose styles correspond to our own. Having a liberal style, I tend to respond well to colleagues who want to overturn the establishment. So the people in my field whom I am most likely to seek out are those who believe that the IQ testing business is misguided and who believe that new, better tests are just over the horizon. There are equally good scholars who have done careful scientific research arguing, more or less, for the status quo.

I find them annoying – can't they see the need for new ideas in the field? But the important thing to realize is that my reaction to the field of intelligence as much reflects my style as it reflects any rational beliefs about the field of intelligence. I know this because any field in which I work evokes the same reaction: I always feel that the field needs a major facelift. Others of my acquaintance seem to be happy with the status quo in whatever field they enter.

It is important to distinguish between stylistic leanings and political ones. They are not the same, and in fact, are probably only very weakly correlated, if at all. Newt Gingrich, currently in his second term as speaker of the U.S. House of Representatives, has a conservative political philosophy, but his personal style is decidedly liberal: He is constantly testing the boundaries of the ways things can be done, both in his personal and in his professional life – whether it is with political action committees, book royalties, or how to interpret his role as speaker. His unpopularity in 1996 and 1997 may have been due, in part, to the marked contrast between his personal style and his political views. In the same way, oldtime New Deal Democrats, as represented by certain labor interests, for example, may represent a liberal political philosophy but a conservative style.

Now that we have discussed the nature and some kinds of thinking styles, we will turn in Part II to principles underlying the styles.

The Principles and Development of Thinking Styles

5

The Principles of
Thinking Styles

I'm writing this book because I know I like writing books, and I think I have something to say. I have written or edited about 50 books, so it would be safe to say that writing books is one way I like using my abilities. There are other psychologists who have never written any books, and who would be reluctant to write one. The fact that I like writing books and they don't doesn't mean that I write good books, or that they would write bad ones. This fact leads us to the first of 15 general points you need to understand about thinking styles before we proceed any further. These points will serve as the foundation for much of the rest of the book, and we will return to them again and again.

These points apply to my own theory and to many other theories as well. At the same time, here, as elsewhere, there are honest disagreements among theorists. Hence I cannot claim that everyone in the field would agree with every point I make.

1. *Styles are preferences in the use of abilities, not abilities themselves.* If there were no difference between styles and abilities, we would not need the concept of styles at all: It would be redundant with the concept of abilities. And in fact, some styles have been discounted when it has been found that they are indistinguishable from abilities.

The distinction is an important one. I have had people working with me who had a style that led them to want to create, but whose creations were not particularly good. They were frustrated researchers, in much the same way that people who want to be doctors but who can't stand the sight of blood are frustrated in realizing their career goal.

For example, Mary came to work in our group, highly recommended for her enthusiasm and excitement about doing research in psychology and education. And no one questioned her enthusiasm or excitement. But there was a problem: Mary's abilities mismatched her styles. Mary liked doing creative work, but she really didn't have the creative abilities to do it well. Creative abilities, like other kinds of abilities, are modifiable, but even with the possibility of improvement, Mary had a long way to go.[1] Mary eventually left us to pursue another line of work, in which she is doing well. Today she manages a small business. Some might have viewed it as a failure – Mary didn't make it in graduate school. I viewed it as a success – she found something that was a better match for her styles of thinking.

We've also seen the exact reverse of Mary's situation – someone who has the creative abilities but not the style to match. Dan had done published research as a college student, and when he came to graduate school, everyone had high expectations for him, including Dan himself. He was full of good ideas. But for Dan, as for Mary, there was a problem: He didn't like being creative. In particular, he didn't want to take the kinds of risks that creative people need to take.[2] Like Alex in Chapter 1, Dan was more comfortable if someone else gave him the problem, and he then proceeded to solve it. Dan eventually became a first-rate consultant, working with businesses to solve their problems.

In sum, we need carefully to distinguish styles from abilities, and realize that people's styles may or may not match their abilities, which leads us to our next point.

2. *A match between styles and abilities creates a synergy that is more than the sum of its parts.* Mary and Dan were examples of people whose styles and abilities mismatched each other, resulting in their feeling frustrated with the difference between what they liked to do and what they did well. On the other hand, things ended up well for both of them. Part of maturation is coming to terms not only with who you want to be, but also with who you realistically can be. Mary and Dan found uses of their styles that made sense, given their talents, and vice versa. Not everyone does.

People with exceptional creative but not analytical abilities who like to be creative, or people with exceptional analytical but not creative abilities who like to analyze, are obviously going to be at an advantage over people with creative abilities who prefer to analyze, or people with analytical abilities who like to create. Styles should be understood because they are as important to the quality of the work we do, and to our enjoyment of this work, as are abilities.

José was a successful software designer in a firm that specializes in technological research and development. He was frustrated in his work, though. On the one hand, he had a real knack for coming up with good ideas for new software. On the other hand, what he really wanted to do was manage, not design. He never viewed himself as a software designer, but rather as an executive – the person who takes charge of the software designers. To José, software design was simply a means to an end – the executive suite.

Eventually, José was promoted into management. He was thrilled, because he saw this promotion as the start of the career track in which he was really interested. Five years later, José was still waiting for his trek to the executive suite to start moving into fast forward. The problem was that José wasn't a particularly good manager. He was somewhat disorganized, random in his thinking, and too much of a loner to take the kind of interest in his subordinates that they needed in order to want to go to bat for him. The same attributes that had worked quite well in software design held him back in management. The fast-track software designer had entered the slow track to the executive suite – the very slow track, to be exact.

José, unlike Mary and Dan, never came to terms with the mismatch between what he liked to do and what he did well. The mismatch between styles of thinking and abilities resulted in his being frustrated both as a software designer and as a manager. Unfortunately, José never viewed his problem as one of a mismatch between what he liked to do and what he did well. Rather, he viewed the problem as one of intransigent executives trying to hold back his career. As a result, he never was happy with his lot in life.

3. *Life choices need to fit styles as well as abilities.* Every generation of college students has its preferred career paths. No one could doubt that in the year of my graduation, 1972, law was the prestige career. More than half of my graduating class at Yale is said to have gone on to law school. In those days, law was seen as the career that best combined prestige, challenge, income, and, possibly but by no means certainly, excitement.

I went to my 15th college reunion, and the place was swarming with lawyers. There were corporation lawyers, litigation lawyers, publishing lawyers, and even a few public-interest lawyers. What was really impressive, though, was not the number of lawyers, but how many of them were unhappy with their careers. Many of the unhappy ones had chosen the career not because it was a good match to either their styles or abilities, but because it was the road to riches at the time. The result of this less than reflective choice was a lifetime of career dissatisfaction.

Obviously, their situations could have been worse. Almost without exception, they were making a lot of money. But the same money that allowed them to live well also trapped them in a career that didn't really interest them. They now needed the money in order to maintain their life styles. Even switching to a different and potentially more interesting career would often have meant a steep salary cut, something none of them seemed to relish.

The point is not that there is anything particularly wrong with law as a profession. It's no better or worse, in principle, than any other profession. Rather, the point is that people who enter an occupation not because it is a good match to their abilities and styles but because it is what society or their parents or their superegos want them to do often end up unhappy and unfulfilled. In contrast, those who enter an occupation because it is a good match can easily end up near or at the top of the scale in terms of career satisfaction.

Not all the people who sought high incomes were unhappy. Some of them were delighted with their careers. And they all had in common that they were the people who really wanted to go into their occupations for what they would be doing in those occupations, not merely for the extrinsic rewards they would provide.

I understand the pressure many of my fellow students felt to go into particular occupations. My mother wanted me to go into law. She was somewhat disappointed that I went on to take a Ph.D. in psychology. When I was graduated, she pointed out that the then-president of Rutgers University had both a psychology and a law degree, and that one could do great things with both degrees. I told her I wasn't interested in law. Then, when I received tenure at Yale, she pointed out that I had now proved to myself beyond the shadow of a doubt that I could do psychology, and that I ought to start thinking about my future: It wasn't too late to go to law school. "No thanks," I told her.

I suppose my mother was only half-serious at that point, but many parents are 100% serious. Any number of the students I teach are going to enter careers not because they want to, but because they feel pressure from parents, peers, or society to do so. They may end up being good at what they do, but they probably won't end up being the best, or even particularly liking what they do, because they haven't found a career that matches their styles of thinking as well as the society's pressures.

Not only careers, but spousal choices can be better or worse matches to people's styles. Have you ever watched what happens when someone who is super-organized and needs to have everything in its place marries someone who lays things all over the place, and then can't find them if they are moved or laid out any other way? Or have you seen or perhaps experienced the frustration of someone who loves to be with others married to someone who almost always wants to be alone? When your styles don't match your life choices, you pay, and often others do as well.

4. *People have profiles (or patterns) of styles, not just a single style.* People don't have just a single style, but rather a profile of styles. A person who likes to be creative may be super-organized or totally disorganized, and may be a loner or someone who likes to work with others. Similarly, organized people may or may not prefer to be with others. There is no unidimensional scale of styles, any more than there is of abilities. People vary in all sorts of ways.

We have a tendency to want to see things unidimensionally. Perhaps it's a leftover of an early-childhood way of thinking, when we exhibit centration – focusing on one dimension of objects to the exclusion of others. So a 7-year-old child will believe that if you pour water from a tall, thin glass into a short, stout one, there will have been more water in the original glass because it was taller. The child attends to the dimension of height but ignores the dimension of width. When we see people one-dimensionally, we are doing much the same thing that the child does. For example, people often like to evaluate others as "good" or "bad," as "active" or "passive," rather than seeing them in all their complexity.

We also have a tendency to see illusory correlations.[3] People who are one thing, we conclude, are also another. For example, we might assume that people who are politically conservative are harsher in disciplining their children, because conservative values seem to go with harshness. Such a correlation may or may not exist, but when we assume it does, we essentially fall into the one-dimensional trap, reducing two dimensions to one.

When it comes to styles, people often do the same thing. They may assume, for example, that people who are creative must be messy (or neat), because creative people should be messy (or neat). Or they may assume that people who tend toward global thinking are not pragmatic, because they're removed from the world. The danger, again, is that two distinct dimensions are reduced to one, and that we fail to realize that people are multidimensional, stylistically and in every which way.

5. *Styles are variable across tasks and situations.* I like to be creative in my work and in many aspects of my life, but not in all aspects. Put me in a kitchen, and I would prefer to be told what to do. Thus, I'm more like Bill (from Chapter 1) in my work, but more like Alex in the kitchen. Like others, the style I show in one task (e.g., my work) may be quite different from the style I show in another task (e.g., cooking).

This morning I was installing a speaker system, and followed the instructions to the letter. My son, on the other hand, never pays attention to installation instructions: Part of his enjoyment in buying audio equipment, or practically anything else that needs to be put together or installed, is figuring out how to get it up and going. As for me, I'd like nothing more than to have the job done for me. Yet the challenge of my work in psychology is figuring things out for myself. This book is one of my attempts to figure out things for myself, presenting a new theory and new measures for understanding and assessing thinking styles.

Styles vary not only with tasks, but with situations. You may like figuring out the route to a new destination when the weather is bright and sunny, and take advantage of your figuring out the route to sightsee along the way. But if it is stormy or icy, you may want nothing more than to be given the shortest, quickest route to wherever you need to go. Similarly, you may like to figure out the route yourself if you are traveling with someone whose company you enjoy and with whom you are willing or even eager to take detours, but want to be told the shortest route possible if you are traveling with someone whom you detest.

6. *People differ in the strength of their preferences.* Some people

prefer very strongly to be and work with others, whereas other people have a slight preference – they can take it or leave it. Opportunities to work with others are one aspect of career choices.

Stanford University, where I received my Ph.D., has for many years had a psychology department with a very strong reputation. But when I was a graduate student, it also had a reputation as being a place where faculty largely worked on their own. There was little collaboration between faculty members in their research enterprises.

At the time, there were two members of the faculty, both in different areas, and both of whom would have preferred to engage in more collaborative work. But for one of the faculty members, the preference was only a weak one, whereas for the other faculty member, it was strong and pervasive. The second faculty member eventually left Stanford to take an arguably less prestigious job, but one in which he would have the opportunity to work with others. He decided that the kinds of working conditions he wanted were more important than the name of the institution. And his preference for working with others was so strong that he just could not be satisfied in a place that did not encourage this preference.

People differ not only in absolute strength of preference, but in how pervasive the preference is. For example, Allen chose to enter the world of high finance, and found himself working in a basement office of an investment banking firm making stock projections, accompanied only by the computer. The problem was that part of what had attracted Allen to finance was the frenetic and often frantic interaction of people working in teams to decide on stock recommendations. Given the choice, Allen would almost always prefer to be with others rather than alone. Allen was doing the kind of work he liked, but not under the conditions he liked. He found himself another job.

7. *People differ in their stylistic flexibility.* If there is a key to adaptation, perhaps it is in stylistic flexibility. No one has the luxury of being in an environment that always supports his or her preferred styles. The more flexible people can be, the better they are likely to adjust to a variety of situations.

When Fred was in the third grade, he had a teacher, one year away from retirement, who was convinced that there was one right way to teach, and that she knew what that way was. She ran an extremely rigid and authoritarian classroom, and rewarded students who conformed to the mold while punishing those who did not. Fred was one of the "did nots." As a result, he was almost constantly a target of criticism and even ridicule, as were others in the class. The teacher was inflexible, with the result that people who did not fit her way of teaching were viewed as problem children.

Fred may have had one too many of these teachers, because he himself later became the same way. Fred was someone who, like Ben, liked to do things his own way. But Fred was definitely at the extreme end of this particular continuum. By secondary school, he was in almost constant conflict with his teachers and his parents because of his insistence that things be done his way. Fred's parents tried to teach him that life would not always let him have his own way, and that the faster he acquired some flexibility, the happier he would be. He needed to learn which fights were worth fighting, and which ones were over relatively trivial matters of procedure that could be done in one way or another without its making much difference. Fred has not learned this lesson easily.

Flexibility is valuable in almost any aspect of life – in school, on the job, in intimate relations with other people, and even in dealing with oneself. Just think of how much more effective teachers could be if they accommodated themselves to the varied styles of thinking in their classrooms, or how easy it would be to work for people who allowed us to be ourselves and to get our work done in ways that are effective for us, or how enjoyable it would be to be in a relationship with someone who fully appreciated us for ourselves – for our own likes and dislikes – rather than for what they would like us to be. The advantages of flexibility are so overwhelming that one wonders why we don't emphasize it much more than we do in our teaching of our children, our students, and our employees.

8. *Styles are socialized.* Where do styles come from, and how do they develop? The answer to this question will be considered in more detail later, but for now it is worth underscoring the role of socialization in the development of styles. Children observe role models, and often begin to internalize many of the attributes that they observe in these role models. Thus, children who observe authoritarian role models are particularly susceptible to becoming authoritarian; those

who observe more flexible role models are likely to become flexible. The single best way to encourage the development of certain styles rather than others is probably to role-model it yourself.

Whether we are parents, teachers, mentors, or employers, our attempts to role-model certain styles of thinking are likely to be only partially successful in transmitting those styles.

For one thing, we are not the only role models our charges observe. It is difficult, for example, to compete with the thousands of unrealistic and often unfavorable role models children see in the media.

For another thing, everyone has his or her own personality. What children become is an interaction between their environment and who they are as persons. We can control, although usually only to a fairly minimal extent, the environment to which our children are exposed. But there are even more severe limits as to what we can do to change who they fundamentally are as persons. Thus we can only do the best we can, realizing it may not be enough to change others into whom we might ideally like them to be or become.

One thing we absolutely need to recognize is that what we say is far less important than what we do. If we want our children or students or employees to express themselves creatively, then we have to give them the opportunity to do so. It doesn't matter much if we tell them that we value their creative thinking, and then criticize or forestall every idea they propose.

From time to time, I do workshops for teachers, parents, and businesses that are eager to encourage open-ended, exploratory, creative thinking. One unfavorable sign is when someone asks me exactly what they should do to encourage creativity. They want me to tell them step by step, blow by blow. Their desire is an unfavorable sign because if they want a recipe for creativity, they won't find it. Moreover, someone who wants to be told exactly what to do is not likely to model a creative style, no matter how much they may wish to do so.

Ultimately, you most encourage creative thinking by modeling it. It is hard to encourage creative thinking if you do not model it.

You also encourage styles by giving people (children, students, employees, whomever) opportunities to work in those styles. It is for this reason that I vary the kinds of assignments I give students. If I want them to develop flexibility, then I have to give them the opportunity to learn and think flexibly in my courses. If I always lecture, or always give multiple-choice tests, I am basically encouraging one small set of styles over all others.

9. *Styles can vary across the life span.* When you start off as a lower-level manager in a typical business concern, you may, if you are lucky, have a full-time secretary, but you more likely have to rely on a secretarial pool. By the time you reach the heights of the executive suite, you may have not only your own secretary, but an entire staff waiting to do your bidding. The kinds of styles you are going to be able to adopt in your work are therefore going to be quite different at the senior levels from what you are going to be able to adopt at the junior levels.

For example, when you're junior, you better pay attention to the details, because no one else is going to, and if you don't, you may find yourself in trouble. When you're senior, you may have a hive of worker bees to pay attention to details that you don't want or don't have the time to address.

The same basic principle applies in many jobs. Partners in law firms have more resources at their disposal than do associates. Full professors typically have more staff than do assistant professors, and indeed may sometimes view some of the assistant professors in a way that blurs the distinction between them and their staff. When you are starting a household, you may do various kinds of upkeep yourself because you can't afford to pay other people to do them; 20 years later, you at least hope to have the funds to hire a house cleaner, painters, or the like.

Styles can change not only because of the changes in available resources, but because you find yourself changing. When I started out on my career, I did painstakingly detailed mathematical models of cognitive performance on fairly specific tasks, such as solving analogy problems of the kinds found on tests of mental abilities. At the time, this kind of work seemed important to me, and the right kind of work to be doing in my own specialization within psychology, the psychology of human thought.

The kinds of things that then seemed important to me don't seem quite so important now, 20 years later. I have trouble remembering why I thought it was so important for me to construct highly detailed models of cognitive performance on specific mental tasks. I can still see the value of such work, but it is not work that I particularly want to do myself. I have become interested in what I perceive as larger questions.

Other people seem to go in the opposite direction, relishing more and more each year the details that once would have seemed unimportant to them. They may decide that the truth lies in the details, not in what they may come to see as banal generalities.

Some job streams have built-in safety valves for those who find their styles changing, and at the same time find their fit to their job decreasing year by year. For example, some lawyers can become judges; research-and-development scientists can become managers; teachers can become administrators; athletes can become coaches. These safety valves are important ways of ensuring that people can find, within their job stream, a set of tasks that is appropriate for them at a given time.

The point is not that everyone changes in the same way, but that many people change with age in their styles of thinking. Styles, like abilities, are fluid rather than fixed, and dynamic rather than static entities. Contrary to the impression I had when I was 21, development does not stop on or about the day you attain majority age. Rather, it is an ongoing process throughout one's life span, and the modes of thinking with which one is so comfortable in one's youth often seem foreign and strange years later.

Because styles do change across the life span, it is important to be cognizant of the fact that the way you think now may not be the way you will think in 10 or even 5 years, and is probably not the way you thought 10 or even 5 years ago. This fact means that we also need to be accepting of others when they think in ways we don't understand. Before long, we may be thinking like them. Many of us who are parents of teenagers know what I mean. The very behavior that I deplore in my two teenagers is behavior that I showed myself at their age. I, too, thought I was omniscient. (Of course, I was, but my teenagers – no way!)

10. *Styles are measurable.* In science, measurement matters. If you can't measure a construct, it is often hard to demonstrate it even exists. Moreover, if a construct can't be measured, it tends to stay in the land of scientific fuzzballs, ideas that may be intriguing but that don't really give rise to any substantive research.

Measurement is equally important in education. If you want to use a construct for diagnosis or for prediction, you need to have one or more solid measures of the construct. The problem in education is that instead of following theory, measurement has often preceded theory. The result is that we end up measuring something, but we don't know what we are measuring.

This potentially disastrous state of affairs is what has existed in intelligence measurement ever since its inception. People have been measuring what they believe is intelligence without having a really firm understanding of what it is that they are measuring. Many theorists in psychology believe that conventional tests of intelligence measure only a relatively narrow aspect of intelligence.[4] The result is that what we may take as a difference between two people in their levels of intelligence may reflect only a difference in a fairly small portion of their levels of intelligence.

Of course, no testing is perfect, including testing of styles. Moreover, whereas tests of intelligence have been developed and refined over a period of many years, the tests of styles described in this book are new and have only recently even been tried. But I have described in the book a variety of kinds of assessment devices, ones that show somewhat more variation in content and form than one typically finds with tests of intelligence.

11. *Styles are teachable.* For the most part, people acquire their styles through socialization. But it is also possible to teach styles.

One way to teach styles is by giving children or students tasks that require them to utilize the styles you want to develop. That's why I give my own students a wide variety of instructional activities – lectures, in-class discussions, small-group exercises, exams, papers, homework assignments, and the like. The more that people use a particular style, the more comfortable they become with its use.

Another way to teach styles is by teaching the theory in this book (or another theory, if you prefer!). When students learn directly about styles, they come to realize that they have more options than they may have thought, and moreover, that because someone thinks in a way that is different from the way they think, it does not mean that the person thinks more poorly (or better). Many students gain a sense of self-efficacy when they learn about styles, because they realize that there is nothing wrong with the way they think. What is important is to make the most of it.

12. *Styles valued at one time may not be valued at another.* Remember our discussion in Chapter 1 of students taking an introductory

course in a certain area: Those who get A's are not necessarily the best in the career that follows from the course. Throughout the life span, the styles that are required for success at various points of career change.

When children are in nursery school and kindergarten, they are typically encouraged to engage in exploratory play and other inquiry activities. They are on their way toward developing a creative mode of thinking about the world in which they live. But they are also being prepared for the next step via, of all things, coloring books. They are learning that in life, as in coloring books, they will be expected to stay within the lines.

When children enter elementary school, some of those who were most successful in nursery school and kindergarten may start looking only so-so, whereas others who did not particularly thrive in the unstructured environments of the nursery school and kindergarten may find themselves thriving. Year by year, the environment typically becomes more and more structured. Children are taught the rules for reading, the rules for doing arithmetic, the rules for writing, the rules of the classroom, and the rules that society expects them to obey. By the time they are in high school, kindergarten is at best a distant memory, and so are the styles that were valued in the kindergarten.

The activities of the workplace may differ quite a bit from the activities of the school, and often, the abilities required for success in a job are quite different from those required for success in school. But most jobs have in common with secondary school, college, and coloring books the demand that the individual stay within the lines. Not all jobs are this way: for example, creative writer, artist, or even research scientist. It is perhaps no wonder that the best creative writers and artists are often people who did not do particularly well in school.

The ones who did particularly well, say, in high school or college English are more likely to become the literary scholars and critics than literary writers. These academic successes continue to do in their careers what they did so well in school – critique. Indeed, in some colleges, creative writing, if it is done at all, is done in a separate department that is distinct from the English (or comparative literature) department. Having such a department is, in my opinion, a blessing, because it allows those who like to do creative writing to find an outlet that they otherwise might not have in a college setting. Similarly, the people who become musicians are not the same ones who become music critics, nor are the ones who become artists the same ones who become art critics.

Many people find that their success in their career waxes and wanes, and a part of what causes this waxing and waning may be the fit of thinking styles to job requirements at a given stage of career. Consider, for example, managers in business. Ask yourself what an organization generally wants when it hires an entry-level manager: Typically, what the organization wants is someone who will do what he or she is told to do; who will not ask questions about why it should be done, or why it should be done in the way it is done; and who gets it done without letting anything get in the way.

But now ask yourself what an organization generally wants in a higher-level manager. Now, they are likely to want not someone who will simply do what he or she is told, but someone who will know what to tell other people to do; who will ask whether the organization is doing the right things, and doing them in the right way; and who will stop doing what he or she is doing if other things of higher priority need to be attended to first.

Observe that the styles of thinking that are desired at the higher levels of management are, in many respects, the opposite of the ones that are desired at the lower levels. This fact has an unhappy implication if one asks who is likely to be promoted from the lower to the upper levels of management, or if one asks who, on the other hand, is likely to be derailed. Typically, the people who are promoted are those who do their job well at the lower levels of the totem pole; the ones who don't do their job the way they are supposed to are those who are likely to be derailed.

The result of this filtering process is that we may literally promote up into the higher levels of management exactly those people who are least appropriate for jobs at the higher levels. Of course, to the extent that someone is flexible, that person will be able to accommodate better to the styles of thinking required at any level of management, or of anything else. But no one is completely flexible. The result is that we risk losing those whom later we will most need, and of keeping those of whom we will later have the least need.

We frequently see references to the "Peter principle" in the literature on management, reflecting the idea that people are often promoted to their level of incompetence. But the notion of styles leads us to a somewhat different conclusion. The problem may not be one of competence or ability, but rather of the match between a person's style and the requirements of jobs at different levels in the job stream. We may be promoting people not into jobs for which they are incompetent, but rather into jobs for which their styles are no longer a good match.

The problem of shifting stylistic requirements can be seen particularly well in the transitions that occur as organizations mature. A start-up company that is successful gradually transforms itself into a more mature and typically more hierarchical organization. In some cases, a management bureaucracy grows along with the management hierarchy. Not infrequently, those who started the company either decide to leave voluntarily or are forced out of the company that they started. The irony of this kind of event is lost on practically no one: The person who founded the organization is now found to be irrelevant, or even detrimental to it.

From the standpoint of a theory of styles, such an event is neither surprising nor likely to be unusual. The styles of thinking that are compatible with rugged entrepreneurship are often not the styles that are compatible with management in a more entrenched and possibly bureaucratic firm. Similarly, different styles may be required for different levels of kinds of responsibility in an organization. Viewing this incompatibility in terms of abilities is, in my opinion, foolish. The start-up entrepreneur has no lack of ability; if he or she had, the company never would have succeeded in the first place. Rather, the individual has a revolutionary spirit that is more suitable to the earlier than to the later stages of organizational development. What had worked so well earlier on simply no longer works. If the person cannot be flexible, he or she is likely to find it hard to fit into the organization.

Often, there is more flexibility as one advances in a career. For example, in the lower levels of some hierarchies, individuals have to prove their worth as individuals, even if they are working in teams. Advancement means that the individual has proven his or her mettle. People who are not careful to show their value to the organization may find themselves sidetracked.

One can see this problem in science. Much of science is done collaboratively. But in order to get promoted up through the ranks, one has to show that one has creative, productive ideas. Doing everything collaboratively, especially if the same team is always involved, can result in the individual's own contributions being unclear, and possibly can be detrimental to advancement. As science becomes more and more expensive to do, and as there are fewer and fewer sources of funding for scientific work, it becomes harder and harder to show what one can accomplish. These are tough times for aspiring young scientists.

13. *Styles valued in one place may not be valued in another.* Anyone who teaches has had the experience of giving the very same lesson to two (or more) different classes, and finding that the very same lesson that went so well with one class now goes terribly with another. The phenomenon can happen in any class, small or large. Many years, I teach the introduction to psychology course for college freshmen and sophomores. I am likely to find myself using many of the same lectures and many of the same jokes. But the same jokes that inspire howls of laughter in one year's class often don't elicit even a grin in another year's class. In desperation, I once finally put a "laugh" sign on the blackboard, and started pointing to it when I would tell a joke that got a rise out of no one.

The phenomenon is not limited to teaching. Those who give talks, seminars, or workshops also find that the very same workshop that went so well in one place can bomb in another. For example, I give many colloquia to university departments of psychology and education. I know that the very same talk that goes over marvelously well in the psychology department at Yale University is likely to be a flop in the psychology department of some other university, and vice versa. Why? Because the two institutions may value different and in some respects opposing styles of research.

In sales, the very same style of selling that works wonderfully well with one potential customer may totally bomb with another. For example, I bought my car from a car salesman who could not stop showing off his knowledge of the car he was selling. I was impressed: Here was one of the few car salesmen I had encountered who really knew his product. But another customer might be turned off by the endless details. For sure, the best salespeople tailor their pitches to their individual customers.

The same issues matter in the corporate world too. People who fit into companies that emphasize criticisms of procedures or innovative ideas are often culturally far apart from companies that value unquestioning acceptance of company norms or keeping your innovative ideas to yourself. The person who is valued in the first organization is likely to be devalued in the second, and vice versa. What is valued stylistically in one place, in other words, is the same as what is deprecated at the other.

The same principle applies in interpersonal relationships. Many of us have had the experience of being in a close relationship with someone for whom we could hardly ever do anything right, and also of being with other people for whom we could hardly ever do anything wrong. Yet both kinds of people are likely to think that what they value is what really should be valued in an interpersonal relationship. Often, the difference in what they value is a question of style. People tend not to recognize this fact, however. They confuse what they value with what is "right."

One person may feel very comfortable with someone who is highly organized, whereas another person feels bored and cramped with this same highly organized person. One person may love to interact with someone who flits from idea to idea and can never finish a sentence, while another person may feel highly frustrated by the same individual. One person may like someone who is evaluative and often points out the strengths and weaknesses of friends, while another person feels threatened by this same individual. Compatibility in relationships often means finding someone who appreciates not only who we are, in general, but the styles we have, in particular.

We need to be aware that what people or organizations say they value and what they really value not infrequently diverge. One of the more notorious examples was Mao Tse-tung's campaign to let a hundred different flowers bloom, with everyone saying what was on his or her mind. Some people actually took Mao up on his suggestion – and a fair number of them ended up in prison camps. Mao's invitation was his way of spotting dissension in the ranks.

Unfortunately, one does not have to go to China or to the past to find divergences between what is really valued and what is said to be valued. Few organizations would say that they discourage creative thinking, but few organizations truly encourage it. It is not uncommon to be in an organization that values teams, and then to find members of the teams regularly stabbing each other in the back as they jockey for position.

Schools are some of the worst offenders when it comes to matching what is said to what is done. Of course, school administrators will say they promote teachers into administration for teaching excellence. Is that all that matters? If you visit schools, you will rather frequently find one in which all or almost all the teachers are women, but the principal is a man. Now try to find the reverse situation, where the teachers are all men and the principal a woman. Good luck. With regard to styles, upper-level administrators will often say they value teachers who think for themselves, and then promote to a principalship or other administrative job someone whose main claim to fame is willingness to say "yes" to the demands of higher-ups.

Sometimes, interviews are used as a way to spot those who will conform. A woman working in a state department of education interviewed for the number two job in the state, right below that of commissioner of education. She was asked whether she viewed the number two job as one of being an educational leader or as one of being an administrator. Given that it was the number two job, she said "educational leader." Wrong. The job went to someone who gave the right answer, namely, to let number one get all the credit for leadership. Many a vice-president of the United States has been reduced to being a toady in the service of the sometimes ill-fated policies of the president. No doubt about the style that is valued there.

In Mexico, the presidency involves a ritual that is even stranger. In practice, the president selects his successor, virtually always someone who has been a yes-man and who has done what he has been told to do. There is a popular vote, but the same party, the PRI (Institutional Revolutionary Party), has consistently won the vote for years, for reasons that can be debated. The more slavish the individual has been, the better his chances of getting the nod, and then getting elected president. In this way, the president tries to ensure the continuation of his policies. But historically, new presidents have usually turned on their predecessors almost immediately upon being elected. And the attacks have been very aggressive. So the irony is that the person picked to follow in the steps of his predecessor has, by tradition, done exactly the opposite.

14. *Styles are not, on average, good or bad – it's a question of fit.*
When we talk about abilities, we can talk about better or worse, but it
should be clear by now that styles are better or worse only within a
given context. A style that may fit well in one context may fit poorly or
not at all in another.

One cannot judge stylistic fit simply by the generic name of a job. For
example, a professor in one field may do work that primarily requires
creativity, as in one of the sciences, whereas a professor in another field
may do work that primarily requires criticism, as in literature. Of
course, the criticism can be creative, and the creative work critically
analyzed, but the primary styles required in the two positions may be
somewhat different. Similarly, the profile of styles required by a litiga-
tor is likely to be somewhat different from the profile of styles required
by a corporate lawyer who never enters a courtroom. Selling to people
who come to you, as in a dress store, may require styles that differ from
those required to sell by telemarketing, where the telemarketer goes
after people who usually do not even view themselves as customers.

Even within a job, most tasks require a combination of styles, and
many jobs require at least some of almost every style at one time or
another. Hence we can see the advantage of flexibility. What we most
need to recognize, though, is that the same styles that are a really good
fit in one task or situation may not be a good fit in another, whereas
higher levels of abilities are generally viewed as desirable, almost without regard to the situation.

The question of fit is a critical one. Probably the single worst piece of
advice I ever gave as a teacher was to a student who received two job
offers, one from a highly prestigious institution and the other from an
institution of moderate prestige. I recommended that he take the more
prestigious job. Why was this advice so bad? Because I knew, as did he,
that the kind of work he liked to do, and his style of thinking about
problems, was a much better fit to the institution of moderate prestige
than to the institution of higher prestige. Unfortunately, he followed
my advice.

He took the job in the high-prestige institution, and as anyone might
have predicted, just didn't fit in very well. The people in that institution
never really valued what he had to offer. The result was that he became
marginalized, and eventually found himself having to leave. Had he
taken the job in the other institution, I have little doubt that he would

have fit in well, done better work, and ultimately been much happier. The lesson we both learned, but that I should have known, is that what matters most is finding an environment that fits what one has to offer stylistically, rather than an environment that may have high recognition, but that is unlikely to value what one does.

15. *We confuse stylistic fit with levels of abilities.* We finish this chapter, in a sense, coming full circle to where we started. People and institutions tend to value other people and institutions like themselves. The result is that we tend to see as higher in ability those who are like us. As a result, many children as well as adults are never appreciated for what they are, but rather for how they fit into the stylistic pattern of the evaluator.

As the editor of a psychological journal, I have discovered over the years that reviewers of articles for the journal can be roughly classified as falling into two groups: those who evaluate articles for the extent to which the articles fit their own way of seeing the world; and those who evaluate articles for their quality, regardless of whether the writer's way of seeing the world matches the reviewer's or not.

When we evaluate people, we often find ourselves falling into the same two categories. There are those who look for and appreciate only others like themselves, and there are those who look for quality, whether or not it is the same kind of quality they have to offer. We will better utilize other people's talents, and better help them develop, if we recognize people for their own stylistic strengths, rather than for what we might ideally like them to be.

6

The Development of Thinking Styles

Where do the various styles of intellectual functioning come from? It is certainly possible that at least some portion of stylistic preference is inherited, but I doubt that it is a large part. Rather, styles would seem to be partly socialized constructs, just as is intelligence.[1] From early on we perceive certain styles of interaction with others and with things in the environment to be more rewarded than others, and we probably gravitate toward these styles, at the same time that we have built-in predispositions that place constraints on how much and how well we are able to adopt those rewarded styles. To some extent, society structures tasks along lines that benefit one style or another in a given situation. There is a continuous feedback loop between the exercise of a style and how well that style works in a given societally imposed task. It is important to add that some of the rewards as well as punishments for various styles of interaction are probably internal rather than external. We adopt styles not only in relation to external objects and people, but in relation to ourselves.

VARIABLES IN STYLISTIC DEVELOPMENT

Consider some of the variables that are likely to affect the development of thinking styles.

Culture

A first variable is culture. Some cultures are likely to be more rewarding of certain styles than of others. For example, the North American emphasis on innovation and making the "better mousetrap" may lead to relatively greater reward for the legislative and liberal styles, at least among adults. National heroes of one kind or another in the United States, such as Edison as inventor, Einstein as scientist, Jefferson as political theorist, Steven Jobs as entrepreneur, and Ernest Hemingway as author, tend often to be heroes by virtue of their legislative contribution.

Other societies, such as Japan, that traditionally more highly emphasize conformity and the following of tradition, may be more likely to lead to executive and conservative styles. A society that emphasizes conformity and tradition to a very great degree may stagnate because of the styles induced in its members. It is interesting to view the transition of the label "Made in Japan" from its image in the 1950s as indicative of a cheap imitation of an American product, to an image of high-tech innovation in the 1990s. The change in image seems, at least in part, to mirror a transition occurring in the styles that are rewarded in Japanese society.

In some cultures, children are taught from an early age not to question certain religious tenets. Or they may be taught not to question the government. Parents do not, for the most part, want to see their children in prison. In North Korea or China, for example, questioning the government can result in imprisonment or worse, and so parents have a strong incentive to reward a conservative style and to punish a liberal one. In other societies, children are encouraged to question much of what they are taught. I believe these differences matter a great deal. It is sometimes asked why members of certain religious and ethnic groups are so much more likely to win Nobel Prizes or other prizes than are members of other groups. It is easy to attribute the differences to political motivations on the part of the prize-awarders, or to differential opportunities for different groups. But in the case of religions, often the members of the different religions will have been brought up in the same countries and in very similar socioeconomic circumstances. I believe that styles are much of what count: Some groups encourage the kind of legislative, liberal thinking that is likely to produce creative work and to eventuate in prizes for creative achievement. Other groups discourage such thinking, and ultimately are less likely to see their members winning these prizes.

Consider another variable that differs across cultures – individualism–collectivism. This variable has been widely used as a basis for understanding important differences in values between cultures.[2] This dimension deals with the extent to which a given culture encourages and supports the needs and desires of the individual for his or her own sake over the needs and desires of a collectivity. Members of individualistic cultures tend to view themselves fundamentally as separate and autonomous entities; members of collectivistic cultures tend to view themselves as fundamentally interconnected with others. In the collectivistic culture, the individual matters to a large extent as a function of social roles that connect him or her to a larger, group entity.

Matsumoto has described an inventory he and his colleagues use in order to assess individualism–collectivism. People high in collectivism tend to believe it to be more important to comply with direct requests from significant others, to maintain self-control toward these others, and to share credit for the successes and blame for the failures of these others.[3] People high in individualism would be much less likely to show these characteristics.

Hofstede studied 39 countries for individualism–collectivism.[4] The half dozen most individualistic countries, from most to least, were the United States, Australia, Great Britain, Canada, the Netherlands, and New Zealand. The half dozen most collectivistic cultures were, from most to least, Venezuela, Colombia, Pakistan, Peru, Taiwan, and Thailand. There are notable trends. The more individualistic countries tend to be associated with the United Kingdom (past or present) or to be northern European. The most collectivistic countries tend to be Asian or Hispanic.

Although internals and externals will be found in both kinds of cultures, the respective natures of the cultures suggest that internalism will be more highly valued by the individualistic culture, externalism by the collectivistic culture. Why? Because in the individualistic culture the value system rewards the individual in his or her own right. The classic Horatio Alger success story is of an individual rising to the top as he struggles individually and ultimately successfully to work for the system, and to make the system work for him. In a collectivistic culture, the meaning of the individual's life is derived largely through the groups of which he or she is a member, so that it is difficult to define an individual without reference to these external groups.

Gender

A second variable that is potentially relevant to the development of styles is gender. Williams and Best did a study across 30 countries of adjectives that are associated with males and with females in these cultures. There was remarkable consistency in the associated adjectives. Berry, Poortinga, Segall, and Dasen have argued that cultural consistencies in gender stereotypes are so remarkably high that we may have in such stereotypes one of the few true examples of cultural universals.[5]

For example, males were more typically described as adventurous, enterprising, individualistic, inventive, and progressive. Females were more often described as cautious, dependent, fault-finding, shy, and submissive. These stereotypes represent perceptions rather than realities – they may or may not have any basis in fact. But when we socialize youngsters – bring them up to conform to our image of who they should become – we socialize them in terms of our perceptions, not in terms of realities. So if we believe that a male's social role is such-and-such, it is this belief that affects us, rather than the fact that the male's role is actually so-and-so.

The adjectives show, I believe, differences in styles that are likely to be rewarded for males versus females. In particular, males are more likely to be rewarded for a legislative, internal, liberal style, females for an executive or judicial, external, conservative style. On this view, then, males and females will be socialized in different ways, probably from the time they are born. What will be viewed as desirable or at least acceptable behavior will differ between men and women.

There is good informal evidence of this fact. In the executive suite, men and women find themselves faced with different expectations. In some organizations, extremely highly qualified women may be passed over for promotions. In one organization, a woman's advancing herself actively as a candidate for the CEO job was viewed as of somewhat questionable form, but this same behavior was not viewed as questionable when shown by male candidates.

Style differences between men and women can be socialized in ways that are so much a part of a culture that people are hardly aware they matter, such as differential treatment of boy and girl babies from the time they are born. We know that males and females perform differentially on various kinds of tests. A. J. Toynbee comments that, in England, girls used to do better on the 11-plus examination than did boys.[6] But there were more places in grammar schools for boys than for girls. So the problem was solved by enforcing a score handicap for girls – they had to score higher to attain a place in a grammar school. Practices such as this one certainly indicate a differential reward system for the two sexes.

Of course, men do better on some tests, for example, tests of spatial visualization, than do women.[7] It was also noted that, at Oxford University, men are twice as likely to get a First (highest honors) degree than are women. But that's now. In the early 1970s, women were more likely to get Firsts than men. A working report on why this pattern of differences has emerged suggests that women's essay responses tend to be more cautious and conservative, and that this caution works against them when the essays are graded. Put another way, a style of thinking – one that has probably been rewarded for the women but not for the men in their earlier lives – now starts differentially rewarding men and women, such that the women's essays are graded lower for their not taking the risks that they have always before been discouraged from taking.

Because we have collected some, although limited, normative data on styles, we can actually put some of these ideas to a test. How do men and women compare in terms of their styles? Because our samples are small and not necessarily representative, we have to be cautious in drawing conclusions. Moreover, in our data, men and women tended to use the rating scales differently, with men tending to rate themselves more highly on everything than women. Controlling for these differences in our sample of adult laypeople, however, we found men characterizing themselves as somewhat more legislative, less judicial, more global, and more internal. The median scores on the liberalism scale did not differ much for men versus women. However, at the lower end (less liberal), men's liberalism scores were higher than women's –

for example, men needed a 4.1 in order to be at the 10th percentile for liberalism, whereas women needed only a 3.3. This difference did not show up at the upper end. So there was at least some tendency for the data to support our predictions, although, of course, these are only rough data that are far from conclusive.

It is important to realize that these results bespeak what is, rather than what could be or should be. Traditionally, a legislative, liberal pattern of styles has been more acceptable in males than in females. Men were supposed to set the rules, and women to follow them. But this tradition is already changing in many cultures. It is a way things have been done, not a way they must be done.

Age

A third variable is age. Legislativeness is generally encouraged in the preschool young, who are encouraged to develop their creative powers in the relatively unstructured and open environment of the preschool and some homes. Once the children start school, the period of legislative encouragement rapidly draws to a close. Children are now expected to be socialized into the largely conforming values of the school. The teacher now decides what the student should do, and the student does it, for the most part. The choice situation of the preschool – in which the child chooses what to do and how to do it – is over. Students who don't follow directions and the regimentation of the school are viewed as undersocialized and even as misfits. In adulthood, some jobs encourage legislativeness, even though training for such jobs may not. For example, high school physics or history are usually largely executive, with students answering questions or solving problems that the teacher poses. But the physicist and historian are expected to be more legislative. The irony is that they may have forgotten how. We sometimes say that children lose their creativity in school. What they may really lose is the thinking style that generates creative performance.

We change our reward systems without mentioning it to anyone or even being explicitly aware of the changes ourselves. For example, the brilliantly legislative idea about how to run the company might net a high-level executive a bonus, but cost a low-level executive his or her job. The same principle applies in any field.

In my own field of psychology, the system of rewards and punishments changes as one's career develops. In the first year, in a typical introductory psychology course, assessment will be largely in the form of short-answer examinations, at least in the United States. Even essay examinations are likely largely to be spit-back-the-facts types of exams. Students will thus be rewarded, in large part, for an executive, local, conservative style. In advanced college courses and even graduate courses, students are more likely to have to write essays comparing and contrasting theories, or analyzing research or treatment plans. Now, a judicial style becomes important, and the executive style less so. Once the student enters a career, say, as a research psychologist, he or she will be rewarded for creative ideas that advance the field – now the legislative style is being rewarded. People who have been in the field longer are given more freedom to express themselves than are those who are newer to the field. Submitted articles and grant proposals from senior investigators aren't treated in quite the same ways as those from people who are more junior. In effect, the senior person is given more leeway than the junior person to be legislative and liberal and to change the field. Ironically, the junior people are often the more revolutionary, in part because they have not become as entrenched in the field and thus are the ones more likely to have the ideas to change the field.[8] So in academic psychology, as in business, the styles that are rewarded at different times are different, resulting in different people appearing to be more or less competent. The differences are not really in the person's competence, per se, but rather in what is rewarded at different points in career.

A system of rewards may be different for the short and long terms, and the two systems may actually be opposite to each other. For example, work that is very highly legislative and liberal may be initially rejected by people for being too far out. In the long term, however, it is precisely this work that may ultimately be the work that changes the field, and that receives the greatest rewards.[9]

Parenting Styles

A fourth variable is parenting styles. What the parent encourages and rewards is likely to be reflected in the style of the child. Does the parent encourage or discourage legislativeness, or judgment, on the part of the child? The parent him- or herself exhibits a certain style, which the child is likely to emulate. A monarchic parent, for example, is likely to reward a child who shows the same single-mindedness, whereas an anarchic parent would likely abhor a child beginning to show a monarchic style and try to suppress it as unacceptable. Parents who mediate for the child in ways that point to larger rather than smaller issues are more likely to encourage a global style, whereas parents who do not themselves generalize are more likely to encourage a more local style.

I have suggested that one of the more important variables in a child's intellectual development is the parents' ways of dealing with questions that children pose.[10] Over the course of their childhoods, children may ask thousands of questions. Parents react to these questions in a variety of ways, and the ways they react can influence the styles of thinking that their children develop. For example, children are more likely to develop legislative styles if their parents encourage the children to ask questions, and where possible, to seek answers for themselves; children are more likely to develop a judicial style if their parents encourage the children to be evaluative, to compare and contrast, to analyze, to judge things, both with respect to the questions the children ask and with respect to the answers that are given.

This same logic applies to other styles. For example, a child is more likely to be globally inclined if the child has seen the parent (or teacher) dealing with bigger issues, or to be locally inclined if he or she has seen the parent (or teacher) dealing with smaller ones. Encouraging children to work in groups is more likely to foster an external style, whereas encouraging solitary work is more likely to foster an internal style.

Parents, of course, have some but far from total influence. For one thing, children's personalities will differ, and where one child, say, may take more readily to working with others, another child may not. For another thing, other socializing agents compete with the parents and with each other. The parent may encourage broad questioning at home, but the child may be in a school that discourages such questioning. No one socializing agent has a monopoly over the ultimate outcomes.

The religious upbringing the parent gives the child, or, in rarer cases, that the child finds on his or her own, also can have an influence on the development of styles. Some religions, as practiced in the everyday world, are more encouraging of questioning and confrontation than are others. Nobel Prizes are not distributed among various religious groups in proportion to their share of the world population. The pattern of difference is reflective of the emphasis on questioning of existing ways among these various groups.

Schooling and Occupation

A last variable affecting the development of styles is kind of schooling and, ultimately, of occupation. Different schools and, especially, occupations reward different styles. An entrepreneur is likely to be rewarded for different styles than is an assembly-line worker. As individuals respond to the reward system of their chosen life pursuit, various aspects of style are more likely to be either encouraged or suppressed.

On average, schools in most parts of the world are probably most rewarding of the executive, local, conservative style. Children are viewed as "bright" when they do what they are told and do it well. Schools see themselves as socializing agents, but in the sense that the children are to learn how things are thought about and done in the culture; it is relatively rare that a great deal of intellectual independence is encouraged, at least until the very highest levels of schooling, such as advanced graduate or postdoctoral work. Even there, legislative thinking is often not particularly encouraged.

STYLES AND ABILITIES

Obviously, the variables described above are only a sampling rather than a complete listing of those variables that are likely to influence style. Moreover, any discussion such as this one inevitably simplifies the complexities of development, if only because of the complex interactions that occur among variables. Moreover, styles interact with abilities. Occasionally one runs into legislative types who are uncreative, creative people who eschew legislativeness and hierarchies, and so on. But for the most part, the interactions will be more synchronous in well-adjusted people. According to the triarchic theory of human intelligence, contextually intelligent people are ones who capitalize on their strengths and who either remediate or compensate for their weaknesses.[11] A major part of capitalization and compensation would seem to be in finding harmony between one's abilities and one's preferred styles. People who cannot find such harmony are likely to be frustrated by the mismatch between how they like to perform and how they are able to perform.

If styles are indeed socialized, even in part, then they are almost certainly modifiable to at least some degree. Such modification may not be easy. We know little about how to modify thinking, and we know even less about how to modify thinking styles. Presumably, when we learn the mechanisms that might plausibly underlie such attempts at modification, we will pursue a path similar to that some educators and psychologists are using in teaching thinking.[12]

We need to teach students to capitalize upon their strengths, and to remediate and compensate for their weaknesses. Some remediation of weaknesses is almost always possible, but full remediation may not be. Mechanisms of compensation can usually be worked out that help narrow the gap between weak and strong areas of performance. For example, a business executive who does not like detail work may hire someone else to do it for him or her. Ultimately, we can hope that a theory of thinking styles will serve not only as a basis for tests of such styles, but also as a basis for training that maximizes people's flexibility in their encounters with things, others, and themselves.

For example, two scientists come to mind, both of whom are sometimes thought of as somehow being underachievers in their chosen occupation. The theory of styles has something to say about why this might be true. One of the individuals is clearly a judicial type: He enjoys writing critiques, reviewing and editing articles, serving on grant evaluation panels, and the like. But in science, the greatest rewards come not for judicial activities but for legislative ones – for coming up with ideas for theories, experiments, and so on. Similarly, the second scientist seems greatly to enjoy collecting his own data, analyzing it, and writing articles, but seems less interested in the experiments he actually runs. His executive penchant might be more rewarded in a field where the rewards are for executing the ideas of others, rather than for coming up with one's own ideas. But in science, executive and judicial processes must be used in service of legislative ones, as when one plans to conduct and analyze experiments.

In general, different styles may work differentially well at various points within a given career path. Lower-level managers, for example, need to be more executive in style, but higher levels of management call for more legislative and judicial functioning. The fact that stylistic needs may change as a function of level of career raises serious issues about how we select and filter people through career ladders.

One often sees in research and development centers, for example, people who are brilliant engineers but who have nowhere to go within the organization in terms of engineering. They become managers, but less than successful ones. Some of the new biotechnology firms faced this problem as they found that their scientists were not always the best managers, but that managers without scientific backgrounds did not always understand the minds of the scientists. This is not surprising, as managers may tend to be more executive and scientists more legislative.

Some occupations have optional career-path switches built in to accommodate those whose styles do not quite match their jobs. So, for example, lawyers of a more judicial bent may become judges later in their careers. Executive-minded scientists or engineers may become managers in research and development organizations or administrators in universities. Often, in the university setting, administrators have trouble going back to research after their administrative stint has ended; they have discovered that they are, in fact, more executive than, say, legislative in their bent. But being of a certain type at the wrong time in one's career can be fatal. For example, unless the scientist has some legislative ability, he or she may never secure tenure and hence never make it into the administrative ranks within the university. Or a manager who is too judicial early in his or her career may end up stepping on so many toes by judging peers and even superiors that he or she never makes it to the higher ranks, where such judgments might be more appropriate occupationally.

Although I have emphasized how people bring certain styles to jobs, it is important to realize that jobs may also affect and possibly modify styles. A legislative school teacher who tries a stint in administration may find him- or herself gravitating toward an executive style out of necessity, and may increase his or her executive penchant or even abilities. Leaving the legislative (or any other) style for a number of years may actually suppress the style. Just as the job one holds affects one's level of various mental abilities, so may thinking styles. Sometimes the switch may be crucial. Many state and federal legislators, for example, have been lawyers. They may thus actually not be the individuals who would be most comfortable in coming up with new ideas. Indeed, in listening to political speeches of legislators, one is often less than impressed with the freshness of the ideas. Some of these legislators will hire staff to come up with ideas for them, and will then essentially become the mouthpieces for the staff, at the same time receiving credit for the staff's ideas. Other legislators may gravitate toward the legislative style, and come up with their own ideas. The notion of style makes us consider seriously what kinds of job switches are likely to work better, and what kinds are likely not to work so well.

The issues that apply to jobs apply as well to schools. I would argue that many schools most reward executive types – children who work within existing rule systems and seek the rewards that the schools value. To some extent, schools can create executive types out of people who might have been otherwise. But whether the rewards will continue indefinitely for the executive types will depend in part upon career path, creating one reason why school grades are not very predictive of job success. One's ability to get high grades in math courses involving problem solving, for example, probably will not be highly predictive of one's success as a mathematician, an occupation in which many of the rewards are for coming up with the ideas for the problems in the first place. Judicial types may be rewarded somewhat more in secondary and especially in tertiary schooling, where at least some judgmental activity is required, as in solving proofs given by the teacher. Legislative types, if they are rewarded at all, may not be rewarded until graduate school, where there is a need to come up with one's own ideas in dissertation and other research. But some professors – those who want students who are clones, or at least disciples of themselves – may not reward legislative types even in graduate school, preferring executive types who will carry out their work in an effective, diligent, and non-threatening way.

The fit between student and teacher, as between principal and teacher, can be critical to the success of the teacher-student system, or of the principal-teacher system. A legislative student and an executive teacher, for example, may not get on well at all. The legislative student may not even get along with the legislative teacher if that teacher happens to be one who is intolerant of other people's legislativeness. Educators need to take into account their own style in order to understand how it influences their perceptions of and interactions with others, and to clear away their own prejudices.

Clearly, certain children benefit from certain styles. A gifted executive-type student might benefit more from acceleration, where the same material is presented at a more rapid pace. A gifted legislative-type student might benefit more from enrichment, where the opportunity to do creative projects would be consistent with the student's preferred style of working.

It is necessary that schools take into account not only fit between teacher and student (or principal and teacher) style, but also the fit between the way a subject is taught and the way a student thinks. A given course often can be taught in a way that is advantageous (or disadvantageous) to any given style. Consider, for example, an introductory or low-level course in the natural or social sciences. This course might stress learning and using existing facts, principles, and procedures (an executive style of teaching), or it might stress designing a research project (a legislative style of teaching), or it might stress writing papers evaluating theories, experiments, and the like (a judicial style of teaching). Little wonder I received a grade of C in my introductory psychology course, taught in the executive style! And, in retrospect, little wonder that as a professor in my own psychology courses, I used to have a tendency to make the final grade heavily dependent upon the design of a research project. My style of teaching was reflecting my own style of thinking, as is the case with most teachers. The general principle of style of teaching reflecting the teacher's thinking style is not limited to psychology or even science. Writing, for example, might be taught in a way that emphasizes critical (judicial) papers, creative (legislative) papers, or expository (executive) papers.

Sometimes, there is a natural shift in the nature of subject matter over successive levels of advancement, just as there is in jobs. In mathematics and basic sciences, for example, lower levels are clearly more executive, requiring solution of prestructured problems. Higher levels are more clearly legislative, requiring formulation of new ideas for proofs, theories, and experiments. What is of concern is that some of the students screened out in the earlier phases of education might actually succeed quite well in the later ones, and some of the students who succeed in the earlier levels may not be ideally suited to the work of later levels.

Perhaps the most important point to be made is that we tend to confuse level with style of thinking. For example, most current intelligence and achievement tests reward the executive style by far the most – they require solution of prestructured problems. One cannot create one's own problems, or judge the quality of problems on the test (at least not at the time of the test!). Judicial types get some credit for analytical items, but legislative types hardly benefit at all from existing tests, and may actually be harmed by them. Clearly, style will affect perceived competence, but as noted earlier, style is independent of intelligence, in general, although not necessarily within a particular domain. Style ought to count as much as ability and motivation in recommending job placements, although probably not in making school placement decisions that deal with issues of ability rather than style.

How do styles actually matter in school, and what are the findings of research into thinking styles? These are the topics of Part III.

Thinking Styles in School and in Research and Theory

7

Thinking Styles in the Classroom
What Have We Learned?

We have studied thinking styles in classrooms in order to confirm our view that they make a practically important difference to school performance. How do they make such a difference?

STYLES OF THINKING IN INSTRUCTION AND ASSESSMENT

For those who teach and assess students at any level – young children, adolescents, or adults – the theory of mental self-government implies modes of rendering teaching more effective. The key principle is that in order for students to benefit maximally from instruction and assessment, at least some of each should match their styles of thinking. I would not advocate a perfect match all the time: Students need to learn, as does everyone, that the world does not always provide us with a perfect match to our preferred ways of doing things. Flexibility is as important for students as for teachers. But if we want students to show what they truly can do, match of instruction and assessment to styles is essential.

Table 7.1 shows various methods of instruction and the thinking styles that are most compatible with them. The major point of this table is that different methods of instruction work best for different styles of thought. If a teacher wants to reach and truly interact with a student, he or she needs the flexibility to teach to different styles of thinking,

Table 7.1. *Thinking Styles and Methods of Instruction*

Method of Instruction	Style(s) Most Compatible with Method of Instruction
Lecture	Executive, Hierarchical
Thought-based questioning	Judicial, Legislative
Cooperative (group) learning	External
Problem solving of given problems	Executive
Projects	Legislative
Small group: students answering factual questions	External, Executive
Small group: students discussing ideas	External, Judicial
Reading	Internal, Hierarchical

which means varying teaching style to suit different styles of thought on the part of students.

By far the most common form of instruction in schools is the lecture. College years, for most students, are consumed by lectures. So are secondary-school years. Elementary-school years are more variable, but almost always include a heavy dose of didactic instruction. The lecture form of instruction tends to be most compatible with executive, hierarchical styles. It is compatible with the executive style because the teacher presents material and the student receives it passively in the form that it is presented by the teacher, usually without much thought on the part of the student as to other ways of organizing the material, and almost always without the student's challenging the teacher's choice of content or organization of material. The lecture style is compatible with the hierarchical style because students usually cannot and do not want to take down everything the teacher says, so they have to decide what are the more and less important things that have been mentioned. To the extent that the teacher drowns the student in details, the lecture format may also benefit the local style at the expense of the global one.

When, less commonly, teachers ask students thought-based questions, the rewarded style is more likely to be judicial or legislative, depending on the kinds of questions asked. If the questions require analysis and judgment (e.g., Why did the United States decide to send troops to Bosnia?), the questions are more likely to appeal to judicial students, whereas if the questions require creative production (e.g., If you were Clinton, would you have sent troops to Bosnia?), the questions are more likely to appeal to legislative students. In our own surveying of classrooms, thought-based questioning is quite a bit less common than is the lecture.[1]

Cooperative learning refers to learning in groups. In my own days as a student, it was usually referred to simply as "group work." The idea is that students will learn more working together in groups than they will individually. Cooperative learning has become, for some, a bit of a panacea, and Slavin argues that it is better for all students than is individual learning.[2] Is it?

From the standpoint of the theory of thinking styles, few methods of instruction are likely to be better for everyone. They may be better, on average, but averages hide individual differences. Cooperative learning is likely to appeal considerably more, for example, to external than to internal students, because externals enjoy working in groups and actively seek them out, whereas internals are likely to shy away from groups and to prefer to work individually. The internal individual, therefore, may find cooperative learning actually to be somewhat painful, whereas the external may find it made to order.

It is important to remember, as stated earlier, that we do not want only to teach students in a way that is comfortable for them. Internal individuals need to learn to work effectively in groups, but so do external students need to learn effectively to work alone. Thus, both groups of students need to learn to work in both ways. From the standpoint of stylistic match and also from the standpoint of the need to vary instructional method, it seems to be mistaken to argue that cooperative learning is always better than individual learning. In fact, cooperative learning is probably not ideal for some gifted children, who will end up spending their time teaching less able students rather than learning themselves.

Projects encourage students to branch out on their own – to formulate their own science experiment, or write their own story, or create their own art portfolio, or do a documentary for history. Projects tend to be particularly welcomed by legislative students because of their invitation to the student to structure the tasks to be done for him- or herself. They leave a lot of room for legislative, creative expression. When they have a number of different parts, or when they have to be sandwiched in among a number of other assignments, they tend to benefit an individual with a hierarchical style, who can fit them in as a priority. In a project such as a master's or doctoral thesis, however, they may better suit someone with a monarchic style, who can put almost everything else aside for a while in order to get the thesis done. People who are not at least somewhat monarchic when they work on a thesis often find it difficult to make the time to get the thesis done.

In a small-group recitation, the student answers factual types of questions posed by the teacher (e.g., In what year was the Magna Carta signed?). The student who is better able to function in an executive manner – basically giving the teacher the answers he or she wants – tends to look better in a small- or even large-group recitation. Teachers often do not realize that such recitations also benefit external over internal students, because they require answering in the context of the group. A shy student may be afraid to speak out, or to assert him- or herself in front of the group. As a result, the student may not speak up. Teachers sometimes make the mistake of believing that internal students don't know the answers, when in fact they are simply afraid to speak in the group setting.

In small-group discussion, students talk about an issue of importance to their education. For example, they may discuss similarities and differences between two books, or why an author might have written a book in the first place. Such discussions favor external students who are willing to speak out in front of the group, and judicial students who like to analyze whatever issue is being discussed.

Even reading is not a "style-free" activity. Silent reading, too, tends to be more compatible with certain styles than with others. In particular, it favors internal students when the students are reading on their own. It favors hierarchical students, because there is usually more to absorb in the material than the student can possibly remember, so the student needs to decide selectively what material is worth learning and what material is not. And it will benefit either executive or judicial students, depending on whether the main goal of the reading is to

remember facts or to analyze ideas. If students are ex
then students with each style will be partially ber

Finally, memorization is largely an executive, '
tivity. It is executive in the sense that one takes exac
one is given and usually the structure in which it is given,
to learn the material as presented. It is local in the sense that it
committing to memory the exact set of details with which one is p
sented, whatever that set of details may be. And it is conservative in
that one absorbs knowledge in the structure in which it is given, much
as has been done in traditional schools for thousands of years.

The implication of this analysis is that teachers need to use a variety
of methods in their teaching. When they rely exclusively or even largely
on a single method, they benefit certain students at the expense of
others. A typical school with a heavy or exclusive reliance on lectures
will benefit executive students, whereas a school like Oxford or Cambridge, which uses small-group or one-on-one discussion with a tutor,
is much more likely to benefit judicial students. Students sometimes
find that they do better in introductory-level courses than in advanced-
level courses, or vice versa. On the present point of view, it is not only
or perhaps even at all because the material is harder or easier, but rather
because introductory courses tend to be taught more in a lecture mode,
and advanced courses tend to be taught more in a seminar mode. The
difference in mode of teaching benefits different styles. Ideally, teachers
would always be trying to benefit different styles equally, meaning that
they would alternate their methods of teaching.

Table 7.2 shows various methods of assessment and the styles with
which they are most compatible. Note that different methods of assessment tend to benefit different thinking styles.

Ability as well as achievement tests in the United States make heavy
use of the multiple-choice format. Multiple-choice testing is very much
oriented toward executive and local thinkers. The structure is provided
by the test item, and the test taker must work within that structure or
get the problem wrong. Many but not all multiple-choice items tend to
go to fairly specific levels of detail. The short-answer format (e.g., Who
was the third president of the United States?) also tends to be widely
used, although more in tests created by teachers for the students they
teach.

The multiple-choice format is often criticized for a variety of reasons,

Table 7.2. *Thinking Styles and Methods of Assessment*

Method of Assessment	Main Skills Tapped	Most Compatible Style(s)
Short-answer and multiple-choice tests	Memory	Executive, Local
	Analysis	Judicial, Local
	Time allocation	Hierarchical
	Working by self	Internal
Essay tests	Memory	Executive, Local
	Macro analysis	Judicial, Global
	Micro analysis	Judicial, Local
	Creativity	Legislative
	Organization	Hierarchical
	Time allocation	Hierarchical
	acceptance of teacher viewpoint	Conservative
	Working by self	Internal
Projects and portfolios	Analysis	Judicial
	Creativity	Legislative
	Teamwork	External
	Working by self	Internal
	Organization	Hierarchical
	High commitment	Monarchic
Interview	Social ease	External

such as that it does not allow people to express their own thoughts or to see things in a way that goes beyond the given information. At one level, these criticisms are correct. At another, *every* form of assessment has both advantages and disadvantages. For example, multiple-choice items have the advantages of being relatively quick to answer, reliable over a long period of time, and objectively scored. The problem is not with multiple choice, but with the sometimes exclusive use of multiple choice, or of any other single type of test item.

Multiple-choice items that require analysis, as in the case of mathematical items, verbal analogy items, or items that measure reading for understanding, tend more to benefit people with a judicial and local style. When teachers (or testing companies) give students more of these items than they can reasonably answer in the time allocated to finish all of them, then the tests tap into the hierarchical style as well. People who can allocate their time well so as to finish the maximum number of items for the given time period find themselves at an advantage. And finally, multiple-choice as well as short-answer items tend to benefit internal individuals who like to work by themselves, which is almost always what they do when they take these tests. Indeed, working with someone else is almost always viewed as cheating.

Essay tests do not benefit particular styles, per se. Rather, whom they benefit depends on how the essays are evaluated. This fact implies that it is important for students to know how they will be evaluated. In my own case, the very first essay test I had as an undergraduate required me to answer brief essay questions. The professor did not indicate how the essays would be graded, and I incorrectly thought that an essay test at the college level meant that the professor wanted us to think creatively. In fact, the test was scored on a 0–10 point scale, with a point given for every fact mentioned that the professor wanted you to mention. So much for creativity. It's not the essay format, but the evaluation scheme that determines who "wins out."

Essays that are graded for memory, as was the one in my introductory psychology course, typically reward executive and local thinkers. If, instead, they are graded for analysis of big ideas, they tend to reward judicial, global thinkers. If they are graded for detail analysis, they reward judicial, local thinkers. If they are graded for creativity, they tend to reward legislative thinkers. Counting organization of the essay heavily tends to reward hierarchical thinkers, because these are the students most likely to use the kind of structured, hierarchical organization that is typically viewed as "good writing." If students are not given time comfortably to finish writing, then again, hierarchical individuals will be rewarded because they will be the individuals best able to budget their time. If what the grader looks for is acceptance of his or her own viewpoint, then the essays will tend to reward conservative thinkers. And finally, if, as is usually the case, students are working on their own, internal individuals will tend to be benefited.

Projects and portfolios (collections of students' best work) tend to reward styles that are quite different from those typically rewarded by short-answer and multiple-choice tests. It is for this reason that it makes particular sense to use both formats in assessing student performance. An emphasis on analysis will tend to reward the judicial style, and an emphasis on creativity, the legislative style. If students work together on projects, the mode of work will tend to reward the external style, whereas if the students work on their own, internal students will be rewarded, on average. As discussed earlier, emphasis on organization tends to benefit hierarchical students, and if a huge time investment is required, then monarchic students may be benefited.

Finally, even interviews tend to reward some styles over others. Sometimes we falsely believe that an interview is somehow a privileged form of assessment – that it can tell us the truth, whereas other measures cannot. So in screening for admission to a school, written applications may first be read, and then interviews may be used as a basis for making final decisions. In hiring people for a job, also, written applications often serve as a prior screening device to select those worthy of being interviewed. Those who do the best in the interview are then hired.

The problem is that interviews are not a privileged form of assessment, and indeed, their validity is highly questionable. They are no different from any other form of assessment in rewarding some styles and penalizing others. For one thing, interviewers will tend, on average, to like people more who are like themselves, as we found in the analysis of teacher-student match in styles. But for another, interviews almost always benefit those with an external style over those with an internal style. Internals may be shy and slow to warm up, with the result that, just as they are warming up, the interview is coming to a close. Unless they are being hired, say, for a sales position or some other position that requires immediate warming up to customers or others, their being internally oriented probably will not be disadvantageous on the job, despite its being disadvantageous in the interview. If the interview is relatively brief, as almost all interviews are, then hierarchical people will be at an advantage, because they will be sure to mention the most important things about themselves up front. And, of course, if the interviewer is looking for someone who conforms to a certain mold, conservative people will very likely be benefited. The point, then, is the interview is just as limited as are any other assessment devices, and should be interpreted accordingly.

Table 7.3. *Thinking Styles and Instructional and Evaluational Assignments*

Style Emphasized		
Executive	Judicial	Legislative
Type of prompt		
Who said?	Compare and contrast . . .	Create . . .
Summarize . . .	Analyze . . .	Invent . . .
Who did?	Evaluate . . .	If you . . .
When did?	In your judgment . . .	Imagine . . .
What did?	Why did?	Design . . .
How did?	What caused?	How would?
Repeat back . . .	What is assumed by?	Suppose . . .
Describe . . .	Critique . . .	Ideally?

Finally, Table 7.3 shows how different prompts in instructional and evaluational assignments can lead to varying levels of compatibility for different styles. Prompts like "Who said . . . ?" and "Who did . . . ?" benefit executive students; prompts like "Compare and contrast . . . " and "Analyze . . . " benefit judicial students; and prompts like "Create . . . " and "Invent. . . " benefit legislative students. Teachers or parents who use prompts that mostly fall into a single column tend to value one of the styles considerably more than the others. Ideally, prompts from all three columns will be used, so that students with different styles will be valued more equally. By varying the kinds of prompts they use, teachers and parents can equalize the benefits to all of the children they teach.

MEASUREMENT OF THINKING STYLES IN THE SCHOOL AND ELSEWHERE

We have used several converging operations to measure thinking styles in school and other settings, some of which were described earlier and so will just be mentioned here.[3]

One such measure, described earlier in the book, is the *Thinking*

Styles Inventory. People are given statements like "If I work on a project, I like to plan what to do and how to do it" (which measures the legislative style), and are asked to rate how well the statement describes them on a 1–7 scale.

A second measure is the *Set of Thinking Styles Tasks for Students,* which measures styles via performance rather than inventory format. In one item, a student is given as a prompt the opening, "When I am studying literature, I prefer . . . " and then the student must choose either "to make up my own story with my own characters and my own plot" (legislative); "to follow the teacher's advice and interpretations of the author's positions, and to use the teacher's way of analyzing literature" (executive); "to evaluate the author's style, to criticize the author's ideas, and to evaluate characters' actions" (judicial); or "to do something else (please indicate)" (scored according to actual response).

In another item from this assessment, people are presented with a scenario in which they are asked to imagine they are the "mayor of a small northeastern city. You have a city budget this year of $1 million. Below is a list of problems currently facing your city. Your job is to decide how you will spend the $1 million available to improve your city. . . ." The students are given options such as "drug problem," "roads," "landfill," and "shelters for the homeless." Scoring is on the basis of allocation of funds. People who allocate all funds to one project are classified as showing a monarchic tendency. Those who prioritize their distribution of funds are scored as hierarchic. Those who distribute money equally across projects are classified as oligarchic. And those who show no system at all are classified as anarchic.

A third measure, the *Thinking Styles Questionnaire for Teachers,* assesses the styles teachers use when they teach. These styles may or may not correspond to the teachers' own preferred style or styles. For example, a legislative teacher may require students to accept his or her ideas, and thus be executive in style of teaching. Typical items on this scale are "I want my students to develop their own ways of solving problems" (legislative) and "I agree with people who call for more and harsher discipline, and a return to the 'good old ways'" (conservative).

A fourth and final measure is the *Students' Thinking Styles Evaluated by Teachers.* Here, a teacher (or other person) evaluates the style of each student. Statements to be rated are ones such as "S/he prefers to solve problems in her/his own way" (legislative) and "S/he likes to evaluate her/his own opinions and those of others" (judicial).

By using a variety of kinds of assessments, we are able to cancel out the biases and errors of measurement inevitably associated with a single kind of measurement, and are thus better able to converge on a more informed assessment of a person's profile of thinking styles.

The various measures have demonstrated good psychometric properties. In other words, they meet the criteria for being "good tests."

One criterion for a good test is that it has high *internal-consistency reliability*. This property refers to all items on a given scale truly measuring the same psychological construct (style). Reliabilities are evaluated on a scale from 0 (low) to 1 (high). Published, standardized tests typically have internal-consistency reliabilities of .8 or higher overall, although scales within the tests may have reliabilities that are lower, such as .7 or even .6. In our work, the 13 scales of the *Thinking Styles Inventory* were found to have internal-consistency reliabilities ranging from .57 to .88 with a median of .82. Only one reliability was in the .50s, two were in the .60s, and one was in the .70s; the rest were in the .80s.

Typically, we have obtained certain significant correlations between styles, regardless of the method of measurement. The global and local scales have always been negatively correlated, as have been the legislative and conservative scales and the liberal and conservative scales. In contrast, the liberal and legislative scales have been positively correlated, as have been the conservative and executive scales.

These patterns of data make sense in terms of the theory. People who prefer novelty and new ways of doing things (liberal style) might sensibly be expected to like to come up with their own new ideas, rather than just accepting the new ideas of others. People who prefer conventional, accepted ways of doing things (conservative style) might sensibly be expected to prefer to take direction, in the cases of conservatives, from the ideas of the past, rather than coming up with their own ideas.

We have also used a technique called factor analysis in order to look at whether the structure of the data we have obtained conforms to the structure that would be expected from the theory. The question here is whether the mental structure revealed to underlie the interrelations among the scales fits the structure that would be expected on the basis of the theory. In other words, does statistical analysis confirm the styles specified by the theory? Several factor analyses have revealed similar factor structures. In one such analysis, we obtained five factors (underlying mental structures) providing a very good but imperfect account of the data.

Factor I, Adherence to Structure, contrasted the liberal and legislative scales with the conservative and executive. In other words, liberal people tend, on average, to be legislative, whereas conservative people tend to be executive. Those who are liberal or legislative tend not to be conservative or executive, and vice versa. This factor makes good sense in terms of the theory of mental self-government.

Factor II, Engagement, comprised two scales, the oligarchic (inverted) and the judicial. This factor was unexpected. It suggests that people who are priority setters tend to be judicial in their way of thinking.

Factor III, Scope, contrasted the external and internal scales. This factor, like the first, was predicted, and made good sense in terms of the theory. It basically states that internal and external people are, on average, at opposite ends of a continuum, and that this continuum is largely unrelated to other styles.

Factor IV, Level, contrasted the local and global scales. This factor, like the first and third, was predicted, suggesting as it does that local and global people are at opposite ends of a continuum and that this continuum is largely unrelated to other styles.

Factor V, Distribution of Time, comprised only the hierarchic scale. It suggests that people differ in the degree to which they are hierarchical, and that this degree is unrelated to other styles.

Considering the five factors in the model, we could fairly say that three of the obtained factors were both predicted and consistent with the model (I, III, IV), one was not predicted but was consistent with the model (V), and the other (II) was neither predicted nor obviously consistent with the model (although neither was it necessarily inconsistent). Thus, the statistical analysis generally supported the theory, although the second factor remains unexplained.

As discussed earlier in the book, there are a number of different theories of styles, some of which seem to cover roughly a similar range of ways of thinking. The styles differ primarily in the models underlying them, and in how the boundaries among the styles are drawn. How are scores on inventories measuring the various styles related?

We have found scores on the mental self-government scales to be correlated with scores on some of the other available measures of styles.

STYLES IN THE CLASSROOM

Elena Grigorenko and I have conducted several studies investigating styles in the classroom.[4] In one project, a first study focused on teachers, a second on students, and a third study focused on the interaction between teachers and students. The schools we studied included a large urban public school, a prestigious secular private school, a Catholic parochial school, and an avant-garde private school with an emphasis on "emotional education."

Thinking Styles of Teachers

In a first study with 85 teachers (57 female, 28 male) in four schools of widely varying types (private and public, and socioeconomically diverse), we found several interesting effects with respect to grade taught, age of teachers, subject area taught, and ideology.

Teachers are more legislative but less executive at the lower grades than at the upper grades. These findings might suggest either that more legislative individuals are attracted to teaching at the lower grade levels or that people teaching at the lower grade levels become more legislative (or that those teaching at the upper grade levels become more executive). The demands on teachers in the United States are consistent with this pattern of findings: Teachers in the upper grades are forced to follow a more rigidly prescribed curriculum than are teachers in the lower grades.

The greater regimentation of learning and thinking in the upper grades is, in my opinion, an undesirable characteristic of our schools. It ill prepares students for college and provides even worse preparation for the world of work, where workers are increasingly being challenged to think for themselves. In our work, we have found that as children progress through school, they show less and less spontaneous creativity in their thinking. Given the demands of schooling, this reduction in spontaneous creativity is not surprising; neither is it appealing, however.

We also found older teachers to be more executive, local, and conservative than younger teachers. It was impossible to separate out age from number of years of teaching experience: There was a very high correlation between the two variables. Again, there are two interpretations of these findings, either or both of which might be correct. One interpretation is that teachers become more executive, local, and conservative with age; the other interpretation is that the difference is due to a cohort effect.

This finding also does not bode potentially well for our schools, in my opinion. The pattern of findings suggests that teachers tend to narrow their focus with age, and, given the pattern of styles, possibly to become more rigid and authoritarian. Whether this tendency is due to burnout, increasing intolerance of deviation from authority with age, or generational differences just cannot be said for sure at this point.

Further, we found that science teachers tended to be more local than were teachers of the humanities, whereas the latter tended to be more liberal than the former. These results again are roughly consistent with our experience. With respect to science, the results unfortunately suggest that science teachers may concentrate substantially more on the local details of science than on the "big picture" of scientific research. This pattern of concentration is not necessarily desirable in terms of preparation of students for a scientific career, where dealing with large, important issues will be a feature that distinguishes more from less successful scientists.

We found that the schools differed in terms of profiles of styles of teachers. Moreover, the differences generally made good sense in terms of the kinds of schools we were studying. With regard to the legislative style, for example, the highest mean was shown by teachers in the private school emphasizing emotional education (6.16 on a 1–7 scale). The lowest mean was in the public high school in the community. With regard to the executive style, the highest mean was in the elementary-secondary Catholic school (4.66). The lowest mean was in the private school emphasizing emotional education (2.33). With regard to the judicial style, the highest mean was in the academically oriented, prestigious private school (5.42). The lowest mean was in the private school emphasizing emotional education (4.82), a school that prides itself on being nonjudgmental.

With regard to the local style, the highest means were among the teachers in the public high school and the Catholic school (4.04 and 4.05). The lowest mean was in the private school emphasizing emotional education (2.58). With regard to the global style, the highest mean was in the Catholic school (5.48). The lowest mean was in the academically oriented private school. With regard to the liberal style, the highest mean was in the Catholic school (5.57), but so was the highest mean for the conservative style (3.68). These results suggest that there may have been distinct subgroups of teachers within the Catholic school. The lowest mean for the liberal style was the public high school (5.08), and the lowest for the conservative style was for the private school emphasizing emotional education (1.84).

We further did an analysis of the relation of school ideology to teachers' styles. We had a rater who was not familiar with the individual teachers in each school rate each school for its own profile of styles on the basis of catalogues, faculty and student handbooks, statements of goals and purposes, and curricula. We also evaluated teachers' styles, and then did contrasts looking at the match between teachers and schools. For six of seven planned analyses, we found significant effects. In other words, teachers tend to match the stylistic ideology of their schools. Either teachers tend to gravitate toward schools that fit them ideologically or else they tend to become like the place they are in. This again suggests the importance of socialization in the formation of styles, even at the adult level.

Thinking Styles of Students

In a second study of 124 students between the ages of 12 and 16 distributed among the same four schools, we found some interesting demographic effects. Socioeconomic level related negatively to the judicial, local, conservative, and oligarchic styles. These results are consistent with a notion of greater authoritarianism in the styles of the individuals of lower socioeconomic class. We also found that later-born siblings tend to be more legislative than earlier-born siblings, consistent with the past finding that first-borns tend to be more accepting of societal dictates than are later-borns.[5] Finally, we found a significant degree of match between students' and teachers' styles. Whereas for the teachers, similarity of styles to the profile of their schools could be interpreted in terms of choice of school, such an explanation is implausible in the case of students, who rarely get to choose their school. The results suggest socialization of styles.

The Relation between Thinking Styles of Teachers and Students

In a third study, we went back to one of the original questions that motivated this work: Do students do better in classrooms where their styles match rather than mismatch the styles of their teachers? We assessed students' and teachers' styles and found that, indeed, students performed better and were more positively evaluated by teachers when the students' styles matched rather than mismatched the styles of their teachers. In other words, the students performed better when they were more like their teachers stylistically, independent of actual level of achievement.

We also looked at correlations between school performance of the students and their styles in the various schools. We found that different schools rewarded different styles, and moreover, that what they rewarded seemed to fit with the stylistic character of the schools. In the public school, the legislative and executive styles both significantly predicted academic achievement (correlations of .36 and .29), suggesting different subgroups of teachers rewarding different things. The hierarchic style also significantly predicted achievement (.29). In the academically oriented private school, significant predictors of academic achievement were the judicial style (.56), the liberal style (.58), and the oligarchic style (.55). In the private school emphasizing emotional education, significant predictors were the legislative style (.52), the global style (.42), the liberal style (.44), the conservative style in the negative direction (−.38), and the hierarchic style (.48). In the private Catholic school, significant predictors of achievement were the executive style (.51), the local style (.39), the liberal style in the negative direction (−.42), the conservative style (.49), and the hierarchic style (.51). Note that correlations range from −1 (perfect inverse relation) to 0 (no relation) to 1 (perfect relation).

Observe that there are major differences among schools, even with respect to direction. For example, a liberal versus a conservative style may help or hurt evaluations of performance, depending on the school. Some schools reward a global style, others a local style. Clearly, different children will be evaluated differently, depending on the school in which they enroll.

Relation of Thinking Styles to Abilities in Predicting Achievement

In a another project, Elena Grigorenko and I asked a different question: When abilities are taken into account, do styles still predict academic achievement?[6] In other words, we were addressing directly the question that motivated much of my interest in styles in the first place, namely, that of whether they account for significant variation in student performance over and beyond what is accounted for by abilities. In this study, 199 high school students from all around the United States as well as from South Africa completed some of our measures of thinking styles. They also took a broad-range test of abilities based on my triarchic theory of human intelligence.[7] Unlike traditional tests of abilities, this test required students not only to use memory and analysis skills, but creative and practical skills as well. Moreover, testing was in both multiple-choice and essay format.

The main task of the students was to complete an advanced-placement (college-level) introductory psychology course taught over a period of four weeks. The course was taught in a way that emphasized either memory, analytical, creative, or practical abilities, depending on the group to which individuals were assigned. Students were assessed for achievement in the course in terms of memory, as well as analytical, creative, and practical thinking.

The legislative and judicial styles were positively correlated with scores on the ability test. The correlations were modest, however: for the legislative style, .17 with analytical thinking and .19 with creative thinking; for the judicial style, .15 with analytical thinking, .20 with creative thinking, and .23 with practical thinking. The executive style, in contrast, was negatively correlated with scores on the test, −.15 with analytical thinking and −.16 with creative thinking.

Somewhat similar patterns were shown in predicting academic

achievement. The legislative style showed significant correlations with the final examination (.14) and with an independent project (.17). The judicial style showed significant correlations with the final exam (.18) and the independent project (.15), as well as with quality of homework (.21). The executive style showed a negative correlation with evaluations of the independent project (−.18).

Let's turn now to the basic question of the study: Do styles contribute significantly to prediction of course performance, after allowing for abilities? The answer is yes. The legislative style and the judicial style both contributed significantly to the prediction of achievement on analytically oriented tasks (with beta weighting coefficients measuring importance of .11 and .09 respectively). The executive style contributed significantly, but negatively. The judicial and executive styles both predicted performance on the creatively oriented measures, the judicial style positively and the executive style negatively. On the practical tasks, the judicial style contributed significantly (beta of .17).

We were also able to see whether, as we would predict, different formats of assessment tended to benefit different students. We found that the examination format was most favorable for judicial students and least favorable for legislative and global students. The independent project was the least beneficial for executive students and also was unfavorable for anarchic students. The project was most beneficial for legislative students. These results are generally consistent with our predictions.

In sum, thinking styles add significantly to abilities in predicting school achievement. We would do better if we took into account not just students' ability levels and patterns, but their profiles of styles as well.

8

A Capsule History of Theory and Research on Styles

Most mathematicians would make lousy accountants. But why? Do they lack mathematical ability? Obviously not. For the most part, they are at or near the top of the scale on any test of mathematical ability that anyone can come up with. Moreover, they were able to become mathematicians only by virtue of high levels of achievement in mathematics, so that they are not people whose abilities simply go unrealized. Rather, they seem to differ stylistically from accountants in major ways. The kinds of problems they like to work on are completely different. For example, few mathematicians would want to learn tax codes; but few accountants would want to spend their time doing mathematical proofs. Accountants and mathematicians may or may not have the abilities to do each other's jobs; what is clear is that stylistically, the requirements of the jobs are worlds apart.

Interest in the notion of styles developed in part as a response to the recognition that conventional ability tests provide only part of the answer to why people differ in their performance, whether that kind of performance is in mathematics or something else. If abilities are only part of the answer to understanding how and why people differ in their performance, what might the rest of the answer be?

One possibility, of course, would be personality. Someone with personal difficulties might well be at risk for various kinds of performances, in school or on the job. But personality has not seemed to be

This chapter was written in collaboration with Elena Grigorenko.

133

the entire answer either. For example, two people might be equally conscientious, but find that they want to be conscientious in different domains and in different ways. Theorists interested in styles have sought an answer at the interface between abilities, on the one hand, and personality, on the other.

More and more, people are recognizing the importance of this interface. The concept of emotional intelligence is one example of this interface.[1] A concept such as social intelligence is another.[2] In the case of styles, though, I believe it is important to maintain the distinction between abilities on the one hand and styles on the other. Emotional intelligence may or may not represent a set of abilities. Styles do not represent a set of abilities, but rather a set of preferences. The distinction is important, because abilities and preferences may or may not correspond, as we find in the case of someone who wants to be a creative writer, but who just can't come up with the ideas.

If we want to start with an understanding of the variety of work that has been done on styles, perhaps as good a place to start as any is the dictionary. According to *Webster's New World Dictionary*, a style is "a distinctive or characteristic manner . . . or method of acting or performing." The more specific term, *cognitive style*, refers to an individual's way of processing information. The term was developed by cognitive psychologists conducting research into problem solving and sensory and perceptual abilities. This research provided some of the first evidence for the existence of distinctive styles.

Styles have received much less attention than they deserve, given their importance to people's functioning. Both successes and failures that have been attributed to abilities are often due to styles. We should give styles their proper due, if only because preferences can be so much easier to mold than are abilities. So what have theorists and researchers learned about styles?

COGNITION-CENTERED STYLES

A movement came into prominence in the 1950s and early 1960s with the idea that styles could provide a bridge between the study of cognition (e.g., how we perceive, how we learn, how we think) and the study of personality. The movement was called the cognitive-styles movement. A number of different styles were proposed, all of which seemed somewhat closer to cognition than to personality.

Field Dependence–Independence

Did you ever notice that some people seem to be able to find objects that are temporarily misplaced, while others cannot? One person can be looking right at missing earrings, for example, and the earrings seem to blend in with the table on which they are lying. Another person immediately sees the earrings against the background of the table. In general, the first type of person cannot see inconspicuous things right in front of his or her nose, whereas the second type of person can see them. In a war, it may well pay off for an infantryman to be the second kind of person, if he wants to distinguish the enemy's camouflage from the background. But at other times, as in appreciating a painting, noticing things sticking out from their background may be a nuisance. Just what is the difference between the two kinds of people and how they perceive things?

Herman Witkin suggested that people could be categorized in terms of the degree to which they are dependent on the structure of the prevailing visual field.[3] Some people are highly dependent on this field; others are not.

The kind of person who is relatively more field-independent is the person who, when on an airplane, can sense whether the plane is level with the ground or flying at an angle – without looking out the window; the field-dependent person needs to look out the window to figure out the plane's orientation relative to the ground. The field-independent person can also look at a complex drawing and find embedded within it a figure or a shape, such as a hidden triangle. The field-dependent person has more trouble separating the hidden form from its surrounding context. Thus, the field-independent person is the one who sees the earrings as standing out from the table and spots the enemy's camouflage against its natural background.

Witkin and his colleagues actually developed two major tests of field dependence–independence, measuring the construct in much the ways that are described above. The two tests are quite different both with respect to the way in which they are given and with respect to what the test taker needs to do.[4]

Is the phenomenon of field independence versus field dependence a style or is it an ability? In order for a construct to be classified as a style, it has to be distinct from an ability. If styles and abilities amount to the same thing, the construct of a style would be superfluous. The research of Witkin and his colleagues suggested that their measures are different in what they measure from verbal abilities, as measured by a standard intelligence test. But there does appear to be a confounding with abilities.[5]

One becomes suspicious of the relation between a style and an ability when one of two complementary styles *always* seems to be better. As mentioned earlier, one style may be better than another in a given situation, but on average, styles should not be better or worse, but rather differentially good fits to different environments.

In the case of field dependence and field independence, field independence almost always seems to be the preferable style. You are certainly better off if you can orient yourself better in a given environment: It's hard to imagine a situation in which you would be at a disadvantage in having better orientation. If you are an airplane pilot, you want better orientation for sure! Similarly, you are likely to be better off if you can find things that blend into the environment, whether they are keys lost in the house, earrings that fell onto the ground, or the proverbial needle in the haystack, for that matter. If a behavioral tendency is always better than its opposite, then the tendency seems to have the properties of an ability rather than of a style.

Finally, the tests used to measure field dependence–independence have the whiff of ability tests: There are right and wrong answers, and the "difficulty" of an item can be computed as a function of the number of problems that the test taker answers correctly. Certainly sounds like an ability! In fact, the preponderance of the data supports this interpretation.

A review of 20 studies suggested that field independence is consistently correlated with both verbal and performance aspects of intelligence, and that the correlations are moderate (.40 to .60 on a scale where 0 is low, indicating no relation, and 1 is high, indicating a perfect relation).[6] A particularly sophisticated study later uncovered evidence that field independence is essentially indistinguishable from spatial ability – the kind of ability you need to rotate objects mentally in your head, to find your way around a new town, or to fit the suitcases into the trunk of your car.[7] Thus, the preponderance of evidence at this point suggests that field independence is tantamount to spatial ability.

Equivalence Range

Some people tend to see things that are even very different as almost alike. Other people see things that are even very similar as very different. Several different names have been given to describe this difference in categorizing behavior.[8] One name, the one I use here, is equivalence range. Another is leveling (seeing things as similar) versus sharpening (seeing things as different), and still another is conceptual differentiation (narrow versus wide). I tend to have a relatively broad equivalence range (seeing things as similar), whereas others may have a narrower equivalence range (seeing things as different). The advantage of having a broad equivalence range is that one sees things as related where other people might not see the relation; the disadvantage is that one misses important differences that distinguish one thing from another.[9]

The equivalence-range construct seems to be a legitimate style, so long as it is used to measure preference rather than ability. Virtually all psychologists believe that as people grow older and become cognitively more mature, their ability to make differentiations increases. For example, what is a "doggie" to a very young child may include not only dogs, but also cats and other small domesticated animals.

Moreover, as people become expert in an area, they can make distinctions that they could not make before. For example, what would all appear to be wildflowers to a novice would appear as a wide variety of different types of wildflowers to an expert; similarly, what to a novice would look like any old chess position would likely be a specific and nameable chess position to an expert. Thus, equivalence range would appear to be a style so long as it measures preference rather than some kind of cognitive complexity.[10]

Consider next a related style, category width, that also looks at whether people see things broadly or narrowly, but from a different perspective.

Category Width

What is the range in amounts of annual rainfall over a period of 10 years? How about the range in the widths of windows in colonial houses? How about the range in the lengths of whales? No one is likely to know the answers to any of these or similar questions. But to a theorist of cognitive styles, the accuracy of responses is not what is at issue, anyway. Rather, what is of interest is the breadth of the ranges proposed for various objects, such as windows and whales. When people are asked to estimate ranges, some of them consistently tend to give broad estimates, whereas others tend instead to give relatively narrow estimates. The tendency to estimate high or low is used as an estimate of category width.[11]

Items such as those described above are found on the C-W Scale, which is a measure of category width.[12] The idea is to measure the extent to which people tend to see categories as being relatively broader or relatively narrower.

People are not wholly consistent in their category width, as would be expected, because it was noted previously that styles can vary somewhat across tasks and situations. Thus, time and the emotional condition of the individual can affect the responses the individual makes.[13] But often the consistencies are more salient than the differences.

Category width has particularly interesting implications when one goes beyond estimates of ranges of lengths of physical objects to estimates of ranges of psychological variation. For example, what is the range of Scholastic Assessment Test (SAT) scores at the University of Vermont; how about at the University of Florida; at Yale? Perhaps even more interesting would be the possibility that people with broader category widths not only perceive wider variation, but also perceive wider variation as permissible – for example, that they believe that students with a wider range of SAT scores could do the work at the University of Vermont, the University of Florida, or Yale. This aspect of category width bears investigation.

Conceptual Style

Of the following three things, which two best go together: whale, shark, tiger? Which two out of the following three best go together:

airplane, bird, train? Obviously, there is no right answer to quiz questions like these.[14] People with different conceptual styles have difference preferences, depending on how they classify concepts.

Impulsivity–Reflectivity

Do you remember when, as a child, you had to solve rows or even pages of arithmetic problems as fast as you could? The idea was to burn the arithmetic facts into your mind so you would never forget them. Or did you ever take a typing class and do timed typing exercises? In both these situations, the common element is that you had more to do than you could do well in the time that was allotted. This kind of situation leaves you with a choice: Should you complete less of the task, but do what you do flawlessly? Or should you complete as much as you can, recognizing that you will make errors?

Jerome Kagan pointed out that people tend to have a fairly consistent style on tasks like these.[15] Kagan has called the style *impulsivity–reflectivity*. The impulsive person is the one who completes a lot of the task, but allows him- or herself to make mistakes. The reflective person is the one who completes less of the task, but is more careful not to make mistakes in what he or she does complete. The individual usually does not make a conscious choice: He or she does what feels natural.

I suppose I know where I stand: When I started my own typing class in ninth grade, I wowed all my fellow students by typing 77 words per minute the first day. Unfortunately and certainly inconsiderately, the teacher subtracted 10 words per minute for every error we made, so that my final score was something of the order of −87 words per minute – definitely a mismatch between what the teacher was expecting and what I was offering.[16]

A number of studies of the impulsivity–reflectivity construct show that it is relatively stable over time and tasks. Moreover, if one matches impulsive and reflective children for age and verbal ability, one finds that the impulsive children make more errors in reading prose, make more errors of commission on serial recall tests (i.e., asked to recall a string of numbers in order, they are more likely to give a number that is wrong or out of order), and are more likely to offer incorrect solutions on problems requiring inductive reasoning or visual discrimination. In contrast, reflective children make fewer errors in word-recognition tests, serial learning, and inductive reasoning.[17]

There also seem to be personality differences between reflective and impulsive individuals. Impulsive people tend to have minimal anxiety over committing errors, have an orientation toward quick success rather than toward avoiding failure, have relatively low standards for their performance, have low motivation to master tasks, and pay less attention to monitoring of stimuli.[18]

Other Cognitive Styles

Several other cognitive styles have been proposed, which I will mention in passing.

One style is *compartmentalization,* which is the extent to which a person tends to compartmentalize ideas or things in discrete categories. A compartmentalizer likes to put things in a box with a label.[19]

I was trained as a cognitive psychologist – a psychologist who studies how people think. But my work is quite broad, and I dabble in a number of areas. I was once talking to a very well-known cognitive psychologist, and he said off-handedly, "You're not a cognitive psychologist." The comment didn't really seem to follow from anything that had been said before, but the guy definitely seemed upset. I didn't fit his somewhat rigid notion of what a cognitive psychologist was, so I was outside the box. He is not particularly unusual. People who cross lines or blur distinctions often make uncomfortable those who like to put people into boxes, and then nail the lids shut.

Compartmentalization can help people organize their world, but it can also result in their becoming quite rigid. In negotiations, for example, compartmentalization often results in talks that stall and get nowhere. As long as Israelis saw Palestinians more or less uniformly as the bad guys, or Palestinians saw Israelis in the same way, negotiations between the two groups could go nowhere. The same was true in the negotiations toward peace in ex-Yugoslavia. Yale and its unions negotiate every few years, and as is often in the case in such negotiations, it is difficult for the two sides not to start believing their own posturing. But as soon as one side or the other is compartmentalized, it becomes almost impossible to progress toward solutions to conflicts.

Another style is *conceptual integration,* which is a person's tendency to relate or hook up parts or concepts to each other to make meaningful wholes.[20] Perry Mason was a conceptual integrator; so was Sherlock Holmes. So are doctors who try to put together symptoms into a meaningful pattern so that they can form a diagnosis. But many people have no great need to make the parts fit together. They can go through their lives with what Reuven Feuerstein has called an episodic grasp of reality, content to let different concepts and different events occur without any concern for their relation to one another.[21] Note that here we are talking about the style, not the ability. The question is not how well the person puts together the parts, but how much he or she wants to put them together.

A third cognitive style is *tolerance for unrealistic experiences.*[22] This style refers to the extent to which a person is willing to accept and report experiences at variance with the conventional experiencing of reality as we know it. This style can take a number of concrete forms. For example, some people with this style would welcome the effects of a hallucinatory drug, whereas other people, low in this style, would beg off. Some people eagerly embrace virtual-reality experiences that plug them into a world of fantasy dimensions, whereas other people have no use for such experiences.

Finally, a fourth additional style is *scanning,* which, according to Gardner and Moriarty, is the extent to which an individual attempts to verify the judgments he or she makes.[23] Scanning, as defined by Gardner and Moriarty, is clearly a style rather than an ability – it refers to seeking verification, not to the quality of verification. But clearly this is a case where a high score on a measure of the style is better than a low score, so that the construct is a bit more like an ability than most styles. We all stand to gain when we verify our judgments.

Evaluation of the Cognition-centered Theories

The theories of cognitive styles were a first attempt, and an impressive one, to find an interface between abilities on the one hand and personality on the other. Many of the studies were done some time ago, and it is difficult to judge earlier research by contemporary standards. Yet, today, interest in the kinds of cognitive styles described above has waned, and it is worthwhile to try to understand why.[24] At the same time, the theories have to be viewed in their historical context, and with the realization that it is much easier to criticize theories than it is to propose them. No psychological theory is beyond criticism, even those that have had the most impact upon the field of psychology.

The main reason is that described above. The styles seem too close to abilities. Isn't it almost always better, say, to be field-independent rather than field-dependent, or reflective rather than impulsive? Nathan Kogan suggested that we might be able to deal with this problem by dividing styles into three types, depending on how close they are to the abilities domain (with Type I styles closest to the abilities domain and Type III farthest away from this domain).[25] But the taxonomy seems more to recognize that a problem exists than to solve the problem. When styles become like abilities, it is inevitable that one style will be viewed as better than another overall, which seems to carry us away from the whole notion of what a style is supposed to be about.

Other problems have been noted as well. A second one is that the classification of individuals into categories sometimes seems to be somewhat arbitrary, and certainly not cleanly dichotomous, as some theorists suggested. People are impulsive or reflective to degrees, rather than just showing one style or the other. Investigators can place people into categories by splitting scores down the middle, but the fact that such a split is used in categorizing people does not eliminate the individual differences that will exist within the two groups.

A third problem is the absence of any organizing theory or model for understanding the styles in relation to each other. Each set of styles is a separate entity unto itself, without any unifying framework that relates, say, field independence to category width, or category width to reflectivity. In this respect, the literature on styles diverges from most psychological literatures, where there has been an attempt to specify a relatively more complete taxonomy, say, of abilities or of personality traits.

PERSONALITY-CENTERED STYLES

A second movement also has attempted to understand styles, but in a way that more resembles the conceptualization and measurement of personality than of cognition. I will consider here two of the main such theories.

Theory of Psychological Types

The first theory derives from the work of C. G. Jung as it has been interpreted by Myers and Myers. In this theory, four basic distinctions are made. The first is with regard to our attitudes in dealing with other people we encounter.[26] *Extroversion* characterizes those who are outgoing, with an interest in people and the environment; *introversion* describes people whose interests are more inwardly focused. The second distinction is with regard to perceptual functions. An *intuitive* person tends to perceive stimuli holistically and to concentrate on meaning rather than details, whereas a *sensing* person perceives information realistically and precisely. The third distinction is with regard to judgment. *Thinking* people tend to be logical, analytical, and impersonal in their judgments. *Feeling* people tend to be more oriented toward values and emotions in their judgments. The fourth distinction is with regard to interpretation of information. *Perceptive* people tend to be more dependent on information in the environment, whereas *judging* people tend to be more willing to go beyond the information in the environment to make interpretations.

This theory is one of the most elaborated, in that each of the 16 different combinations of the types that make up the four distinctions is alleged to produce a different overall personality type. Consider, for example, two types.

Sensing types who are introverts and who show thinking with judging are alleged to be serious and quiet and to earn success by concentration and thoroughness. They are believed to be practical, orderly, matter-of-fact, realistic, and dependable, and to live their outer life more with thinking, but their inner life more with sensing. In contrast, intuitives who are extroverts with thinking and judging are believed to be hearty, frank, decisive, and leaders in activities. They feel real concern for what others think and want, and try to handle things with due regard for other people's feelings.[27] They live their outer life more with feeling, but their inner life more with intuition.[28]

The theory has probably been the most widely applied of all of the theories of styles. It has been used in settings such as business and education.[29] How valid the theory and measure is for these purposes is open to question. A recent review of the uses of the test suggested that the test is not valid for the purposes for which it is currently being used.

Energic Theory of Mind Styles

Anthony Gregorc has suggested a different and somewhat simpler theory of styles, based on the notion that people differ in the ways they organize space and time.[30] With regard to space, people are classified as either *concrete* or *abstract*. As the names imply, concrete people prefer dealing with the physical expression of information, abstract people with more metaphorical expression. With regard to time, people are classified as either *sequential* or *random*. A sequential person likes things to be presented in a step-by-step, orderly manner, whereas a random person likes things presented in a more haphazard way.

Gregorc has devised a measure of the styles, and like Myers, has characterized what people are like who have each of the four possible combinations of styles. For example, a concrete-sequential person likes the ordered, the practical, and the stable. Individuals in this category have a tendency to focus their attention on concrete reality and physical objects, and to validate ideas via the senses. In contrast, someone who is abstract-random prefers emotional and physical freedom. This person focuses his or her attention on the world of feeling and emotion. The person is also characterized by a tendency to validate ideas via inner guidance.

Evaluation of the Personality-centered Theories

The personality-centered theories, like the cognition-centered ones, have received various criticisms. Again, we need to remember that all theories can be criticized, no matter how good or useful they are.

The personality-based theories are more comprehensive than the cognition-based ones. But statistical analyses of the structure underlying the data from the tests that are used to measure the constructs provide only mixed support for the theories.[31] Thus, attractive though the theories may be, the validations of their structures have not been as promising as one might have hoped.

Second, just as the cognitive styles come extremely close to abilities, the styles in the personality-based theories seem to come extremely close to personality traits. Indeed, one might be hard-pressed to distinguish the Myers-Briggs from a conventional, paper-and-pencil personality inventory.

Third, although the theorists recognize that styles can vary somewhat across tasks and situations, there is a tendency in these theories to "type" people, as the name of the Myers-Briggs Type Indicator suggests. Both theories describe people who are certain types, and classify people into groups. Realistically, though, people cannot be as easily pigeonholed as psychologists would often seem to like them to be. Most people, at least, are more flexible than psychological theories give them credit for.

ACTIVITY-CENTERED STYLES

Activity-centered theories of styles are more action-oriented than are cognitive- or personality-centered theories. They tend more to be centered around kinds of activities people engage in at various points in their lives, such as schooling and work.

Learning Styles

Theories of learning styles deal with how people like to learn. Two theories are described here.

Kolb has proposed a theory of learning styles that is intended primarily to apply in school settings. There are four basic types of learning styles in the theory: converging, diverging, assimilating, and accommodating.[32]

The *converger* tends to be an abstract conceptualizer and to be interested in active experimentation. He or she likes to use deductive reasoning, and to focus it on specific problems. *Divergers* are in some respects the opposite. They prefer concrete experience and reflective observation; they are interested in people, and tend to be imaginative and emotional in their dealings with things and with people. *Assimilators* tend to be abstract conceptualizers and reflective observers. They like to create theoretical models, and to use inductive reasoning to assimilate disparate observations into an integrated explanation. Assimilators are less interested in people than in abstract concepts. *Accommodators* like concrete experience and active experimentation, and also like to take risks. People's styles are determined through the Learning Style Inventory (LSI).[33]

Another theory of learning styles that is widely used in education is the theory of Dunn and Dunn. The Dunns' theory includes 18 different styles divided into four main categories: environmental (sound, light, temperature, design); emotional (motivation, persistence, responsibility, structure); sociological (peers, self, pair, team, adult, varied); and physical (perceptual, intake, time, mobility).[34] It is hard to say exactly how the 18 different styles were chosen, or even why they are called styles. They refer more to elements that affect a person's ability to learn than to ways of learning themselves.

The theories of Kolb and of Dunn and Dunn have been primarily used in the educational world. A theory proposed by Holland has been used primarily in the occupational world.[35] This theory, which serves as the basis of the Strong Vocational Interest Blank (SVIB), specifies five styles that people should take into account in making job choices: realistic, investigative, artistic, social, and enterprising. Scores on the styles help people narrow down vocational choices to ones that make extensive use of their preferred styles.

TEACHING STYLES

Although our focus in this book is on styles of thinking and learning, it is worth mentioning that researchers have also investigated styles of teaching. These styles become important especially in light of the fact that different learners will respond differentially to different styles of teaching. What works well for one learner may not work well for another.

One theory of teaching styles is that of Henson and Borthwick.[36] They have suggested six different styles of teaching. In a *task-oriented* approach, planned tasks associated with appropriate materials are pre-scribed. In a *cooperative-planner* approach, an instructional venture is planned by teachers and students collaboratively, though the teacher is basically in charge. In a *child-centered* approach, the task structure is provided by the teacher, with the students choosing from options according to their interests. In a *subject-centered* approach, the content is planned and structured to the extent that students are nearly excluded from the process. In a *learning-centered* approach, equal concern is shown by the teacher both for the student and for subject content. Finally, in an *emotionally exciting* approach, the teacher tries to make his or her teaching as emotionally stimulating as possible. Notice that these styles are not mutually exclusive. They could be used in conjunction with each other, and probably are most effective when they are so used.

SUMMING UP

Interest in styles remains strong, at least in some circles. The reason is the sense people have that styles exist, that they account for variation in performance that abilities do not account for, and that they may be important in a variety of real-world settings, such as the school, the workplace, and even the home. No theory is going to answer every objection that might be lodged against it, including the theory to be proposed here. But the theory proposed in the next chapter is one effort to address at least some of the criticisms that have been leveled against theories of styles in the past.

Although theories of styles differ, they cover a roughly common ground. Perhaps where they most differ is in how useful they can be to us in our lives. Thus, although I would like readers to accept the theory proposed in this book, my main concern is that they realize the importance of styles, whatever theory or theories they happen to accept. If a supervisor or teacher learned from this book, for example, that a subordinate or student was doing poor work not for lack of ability, but for a lack of match between the individual's styles and the expectations of the supervisor or teacher, then I would be content that the major message of the book had been transmitted. So let's now consider the theory of mental self-government, which I hope you'll decide is a useful one.

9

Why a Theory of Mental Self-government?

The theory of styles that has been described in this book is a *theory of mental self-government*. There is one basic assumption to the theory, namely, that the kinds of governments we have in the world are not merely arbitrary and perhaps random constructions, but rather in a certain sense are mirrors of the mind. In other words, they reflect different ways in which people can organize or govern themselves. On this view, then, governments are very much extensions of individuals: They represent alternative ways in which collectivities, like individuals, can organize themselves.

Before going into details, simply consider the concept at an intuitive level. Take Jake. Jake is failing in high school. Intelligence testing reveals him to be of above-average intelligence, so whatever his problem is, it isn't lack of ability. People who observe Jake are struck by his obvious intelligence, on the one hand, but also by what seems to be some kind of internal chaos, on the other. Jake's attention rarely seems to focus on any one thing for more than a few minutes at a time. Even in conversations, he rambles, moving from one topic to the next, and then to another. His writing, like his conversations, is disorganized, the thoughts seemingly jumbled. When he remembers to do homework, he organizes his time poorly, so that much of what he needs to get done does not actually get done. Jake is rebellious in school, and seems to view it as a prison. It would be tempting these days to label Jake as ADHD – as showing attention deficit hyperactivity disorder – except that Jake does not so much have a deficit of attention as a wandering of his attention, and he's not hyperactive. In terms of a government metaphor, he seems to be anarchic. So are many other students who do not adjust well to schools or other organizations, students who will be falsely labeled as ADHD.

Jake's focus is all over the place; Maria's is in one place. Maria has decided to be a doctor, and almost everything she does is in the service of that goal. It is overwhelmingly her ambition in life. She concentrates on science courses, and does just well enough in other courses so as not to jeopardize her chances of getting into medical school. She volunteers in a hospital. She has worked in a medical laboratory over the summer. She carefully rations the time she spends with her friends so as not to interfere with her plans. The rest of her life is subordinated to that one goal, much as all is subordinated to a monarch in a monarchic system of government. In her monarchy, getting into medical school so as to become a doctor is right at the top.

Jake and Maria are rather extreme cases, but other people show many of the same characteristics Jake and Maria show, but in varying degrees. The idea of any metaphor, including that of government, is to help us understand the dimensions along which people differ, and how these dimensions affect their behavior. So let's pursue the metaphor a bit further.

Governments have various functions (e.g., legislative, executive, judicial), forms (e.g., monarchic, hierarchic, oligarchic, anarchic), levels (e.g., global, local), orientations (e.g., external, internal), and leanings (e.g., liberal, conservative). Similarly, styles need to take into account these various aspects of individual functioning. Thus, we have referred to Jake as "anarchic" and Maria as "monarchic."

Why choose government as a metaphor? Why do we even need yet another theory of styles? What is any new theory going to accomplish that the old ones didn't accomplish? Let's consider again some of the problems with the theories of styles that were summarized in Chapter 8, but now in light of the proposed governmental metaphor.

1. *There is usually no unifying model or metaphor that integrates the various styles, not only between theories, but even within theories.* In none of the theories we reviewed was there a strong unifying model. The individual cognitive styles, for example, were generally proposed in isolation, and attempts to relate them have been after the fact –

through statistical correlations between scores on measures of the various styles. Gregorc's model talks about dimensions of time and space, but these dimensions do not seem uniquely or even perhaps clearly to give rise to the styles that Gregorc uses. For example, concrete and abstract thinking do not follow very closely from a spatial dimension, at least as opposed to anything else that might follow from it.

In the theory of mental self-government, there is a clear organizing model or metaphor, namely, that of government. All of the styles specified by the theory correspond to aspects of government, and one could no doubt add other styles that follow from the governmental metaphor as well. Thus, there is a unifying conception of what people are like, and of what aspects of people generate styles. Moreover, government is a creation of living beings. It is something we invent in order to organize our lives. So are styles. They are ways in which we organize our cognitions about the world in order to make sense of the world.

Metaphors are most useful when they serve as guides rather than as straitjackets. In other words, they should be taken seriously; at the same time, metaphors are analogical. They are not identical to whatever it is they are applied to. As with all kinds of analogies, there are points of disanalogy as well as analogy. Ronald Reagan may have been the swashbuckling cowboy of U.S. presidents, but he was not, literally, a swashbuckling cowboy.[1] Computers may be useful as metaphors for understanding minds, but minds are not computers, nor computers minds. Thus we need to view metaphors as guides, but without interpreting them too literally.

2. *Some of the styles seem too much like abilities.* When we talk of aspects of government, the notion of abilities does not apply. For example, domestic affairs (internal affairs) are no better than foreign affairs (external affairs), nor is, say, the judicial function of government more or less valuable than the legislative function. Governments need to handle both domestic and foreign affairs, as well as legislative and judicial functions. Hence, if we think of styles in terms of what governments do, we do not run into the abilities pitfall, which we saw with styles such as field independence–field dependence.

Of course, we can apply a value system to anything so as to make it seem better or worse. Government is no exception. For example, we may prefer the kind of more diffused central government typically found in democracies to the highly centralized power found in a monarchy. But might there be any advantages to a monarchy? As applied to individuals, might those who are "monarchic" have any advantages? I would argue that they do.

Consider Maria again. Perhaps her friends are disturbed that she doesn't spend as much time with them as they would like. Perhaps her parents are concerned she is working herself too hard. Maybe Maria herself is worried about her preoccupation with getting into medical school. On the other hand, gaining admission to a competitive medical school is extremely difficult these days. When Maria and her friends apply to medical school, chances are in fact good that Maria will have an edge. She will have done all that she could to be admitted to the medical school of her choice. In her individual case, it may or may not pay off, but on average, it almost certainly will. And the medical school she goes to will have implications for the rest of her life, as a better medical school enables her to gain a better internship, and then residency, and then perhaps placement in the field. One can like or not like her preoccupation with medical school, but one's affect toward it is a value judgment. Her preoccupation has both advantages and disadvantages, and that's how it is with styles. With abilities, more is better in almost every instance; with styles, it's a judgment call. Having more of a given style gains you certain things and is likely to lose you others.

3. *Some of the styles seem too much like personality traits.* One could think of a government as having a personality, but in a metaphorical rather than in a literal sense. For example, we might refer to an anarchic state as having a "disorganized" personality, or perhaps a monarchic state as having an "authoritarian" personality. But these uses of the term *personality* are not literal. Similarly, when we use government as a basis for a theory of styles, we are not talking about personality except in a metaphorical sense.

Styles differ from personality in being more cognitive. For example, let's return to Maria. She sounds a bit obsessive-compulsive, doesn't she? In the strict sense of the term, she's not. She doesn't, say, wash her hands many times a day, as would someone who is compulsive, and the thought of being a doctor is not so consuming that she would rather get it out of her mind, but can't, as would be the case for an obsessive.

Rather, she has a salient cognitive goal – to study medicine and become a doctor – around which she tends to organize her life. There may, in fact, be personality traits that lead her to be strongly focused, but the focus is a cognitive one, and her tendency thus to focus is a style.

4. *There is no compelling demonstration of the relevance of the styles in real-world settings.* To the extent that the metaphor of government "works," it clearly has real-world relevance, as government has real-world relevance. We may or may not be able to do without field independence, say, as a construct in our everyday lives; we can probably do without it if we subsume it under spatial ability. But we cannot do without government: Every known society has some form of government, even if it is essentially an anarchic one (as in Somalia and Rwanda, when, at various points, central and many regional governing institutions collapsed).

Just as societies need to govern themselves somehow in order to be effective in the real world, so do individuals. They need to marshal their resources, organize their lives, and set priorities for what they will and will not attend to, much as governments do. Thus, the metaphor suggests that styles are useful. Moreover, I have presented empirical data to verify this assertion, data showing the usefulness of styles in everyday life, and especially in schools.

There is now a convergence of evidence to suggest that just as organisms move in the direction of an evolutionary progression whose exact nature depends on the adaptation of various organisms to the environments in which they find themselves, so do organisms move in the direction of increasing complexity and self-organization. Humans have sometimes been referred to as living systems, because so many complex systems operate within us.[2] From this kind of point of view, we have somehow to govern ourselves, whether we like it or not. At the level of the body, there are systems of regulation that determine when and how we satisfy hunger and thirst motivations. At the level of the self, we need to regulate how we get through the day, a week, or our lives in general. And we need to find ways of relating to those around us. Government is everywhere, not just in society.

5. *There is insufficient connection between the theories of styles and psychological theory, in general.* The theory of mental self-government fits into those theories of individuality that view people as self-

organizing systems that actively shape their environments as well as themselves.[3] The active shaping of the environment is key: People are not just victims of the tosses and turns of the environment, as in a behaviorist or stimulus-response account of behavior, nor are people victims of shadowy inner forces, as in a psychodynamic, Freudian type of account of human behavior. People are shaped by, but also shape their environments. The influence is interactive and reciprocal.

These modern theories occur in a variety of domains, such as those of motivation and of abilities.[4] But styles cannot be considered independently of the environment in which they occur. Rather, people actively interact with their environments, and to a large extent shape the environments that in turn act upon them. Of course, there are chance factors over which people have no control (e.g., the drunken driver who, when you are driving along innocently and cautiously, careers into your car). But even when we take these chances into account, how you react to what happens to you is often as important as what actually happens to you.

The basic idea is that humans are not just passive recipients of the action of the environment on themselves, who respond in either adaptive or maladaptive ways to these complex and sometimes inexplicable forces (a viewpoint somewhat characteristic of Freudian psychodynamic conceptions of the person). Rather, people actively respond in varied ways to the environment, depending in large part upon their styles of responding. So one person like Maria may focus very heavily on getting herself into medical school, whereas another person views this desire as only one in a hierarchy of desires, and not necessarily as a particularly important one.

6. *The styles specified by the theories are sometimes simply not compelling.* What makes one theory compelling and another not? Why do some styles catch on in the psychological lore, whereas others are quickly forgotten? Many factors enter into the success of a theory, such as whether the theory is perceived as elegant, reasonably parsimonious, internally coherent, and empirically valid. I have attempted to show that the theory presented in this book has all of these properties. But perhaps what most makes a theory of styles or of anything else compelling is its heuristic usefulness – that you can do something with it. In this book, I have tried to show that the theory of mental self-

government has immediate implications for various aspects of life, such as the teaching-learning process, the selection of people for jobs, and the selection of partners in interpersonal relationships.

7. *There is insufficient use of converging operations, or multiple methods of measurement.* The issue here is one of producing multiple methods of measurement that all converge on the assessment of the same styles. I have shown that such multiple methods can be used in the assessment of the styles derived from the theory of mental self-government.

Why are multiple methods of measurement important? This issue may sound somewhat technical and even arcane. It's not. When you take an ability or achievement test such as the SAT, which is largely or exclusively multiple-choice, you are often aware that some other testing format might have allowed you to show more (or less) of what you can do.

In an English literature class, the students might read *Wuthering Heights*. Some of the more creative might feel that the novel has given them some new insights into the nature of love, or into the role society can play in either supporting or hindering romantic choices, or into the role of social class in society. The students then may get a multiple-choice test on their recognition of main characters and quotes. The students with the more creative ideas are never going to get to show what they can do.

A candidate fills out an application for a job. The individual has various ideas about how she might play a part in the company, and even about possible improvements for some of their current retail-sales procedures. She never gets a chance to communicate any of these ideas, because the questions asked are all background questions, and none of them allow her to express any of the ideas she has.

In both of the above cases, people with creative ideas do not get the opportunity to show what they would like to show. But of course, if the assessments were based totally on the individuals' expressing creative ideas, then other aspects of the individuals – such as relevant content knowledge for the novel or relevant job experience for the new job – would never get assessed either. We always get better information if we assess people in multiple ways, which is what we do with styles. We never use just one measure, because just as styles can get lost if, say, we only test abilities or achievement in one way, so can styles get lost if we only assess styles in one way. In effect, our measure of styles confounds the styles being assessed with the way they are being assessed, just as now happens with the assessment of abilities and achievement.

8. *There is little or no serious research to show the usefulness of the styles.* Again, I have provided research results showing the usefulness of the styles.

There is a fact that readers should know about styles, and it is that theories and research on styles are at the fringes of the psychological world. They have never formed a central area of endeavor for psychology or psychologists. Sometimes, an area is not studied much for lack of importance, say, to people's lives. That's not the case for styles, anymore than it is for love, which is central to almost everyone's life but has also been relatively little studied by psychologists. Rather, there are some practical reasons.

One is the lack of good research. In some areas of psychology, there is a high ratio of theory to data – in everyday terms, that means "big talk, no show." There is a lot of speculation, a lot of printed pages, but little hard data to demonstrate that any of it is true. Right now, many schools are buying into systems for assessing students' learning styles and for teaching the students that have no solid research base at all. There may be "research," but its quality is so low that it serves as little more than a marketing device for those who are pushing their own system of styles. This area probably won't be taken very seriously in the world of psychological research until it stops being dominated by commercial interests.

A second reason for the relative lack of centrality is the fact that styles are at an interface – that between thought and personality. Psychology, like every other field, tends toward territoriality: There are many people who study thought; there are many people who study personality; there are fewer people who study both; and there are even fewer people who study how they interact, because such work doesn't fit into conventional disciplinary boundaries. When psychologists are hired, they tend to be hired in an area, and one is likely to end up with the personality people not wanting a styles researcher because the work is too cognitively oriented, and the cognitive people not wanting a styles researcher because the work is too personality-oriented. So there's not much incentive, especially for young people, to work in the area. The result is that we do not understand nearly as much about styles of thinking and learning as we should, given the importance of the topic.

There is a third reason why styles have received less attention than they merit, and that is that the area is a relatively new one. People have been talking seriously about memory or intelligence or attitudes for thousands of years. Serious talk about styles, however, is a relatively recent development in the middle years of the twentieth century. There just hasn't been enough time for the area to develop as fully as some other areas have.

9. *The theories don't seem to be theories of styles at all, but rather of the variables that affect styles.* This criticism applies most clearly to the theory of Dunn and Dunn, mentioned in the last chapter, which seems in part to specify environmental variables that might affect styles of learning rather than specifying styles themselves. The aspects of mental self-government are styles, which are affected by aspects of the environment that are not themselves, however, styles.

10. *The styles specified by the theories do not meet some or even most of the criteria for styles described in Chapter 5.* Let us now consider those criteria, and see whether the theory of mental self-government better satisfies them than do other theories.

There have been enough criticisms of styles and the theories that produce them to retard research on styles to the point where it moves at a snail's pace. Is it possible to produce a theory that answers all or most of these objections, as well as one based on a metaphor that compares favorably with other metaphors one might use?

Psychologists have used a variety of metaphors throughout the history of the field in order to understand human behavior. It is always tempting to believe that the current metaphor is the final one – that somehow, although we have made mistakes in the past, we have at last arrived at the truth. This curious point of view does not only apply in science: There was a period a few years ago when people were talking and writing about "the end of history," as though, after the cold war, we had finally settled into the stable and more or less peaceful period of which humanity has always dreamed. Not likely. My own view is that scientific theories and models are always in a state of development, and that if there are any final ones, we have yet to see them, and most likely never will. The evolution in metaphors is, in a sense, dialectical.[5]

First a metaphor or a theory is proposed, and perhaps it catches on. The thesis seems to answer all the important questions people have. After a while, though, people begin to see its weaknesses and its incompleteness. Sometimes, they just get sick of it. So they propose a metaphor or a theory that is, in many respects, the antithesis of the original thesis. Now they see that the first set of ideas was seriously deficient, and so they seek correctness, and even comfort, by going to the opposite extreme. That first set of ideas has been exposed, and the truth has come out at last. But eventually, the new set of ideas is revealed to have its own weaknesses, just as the earlier set of ideas did. So people seek a synthesis between the two, recognizing that although neither set of ideas is perfect, each has strengths upon which a new set of ideas can draw. Eventually, this new set of ideas becomes the new thesis, which, too, will later be replaced by its apparent antithesis.

In psychology, there have been many stages of dialectical development of ideas. Consider just a few of these.

For example, at the turn of the century, a movement called *structuralism* was dominant in psychology: Psychologists believed that all perceptions could be decomposed into elementary constituents – the atoms of perception. The underlying metaphor was an atomic one – an idea that goes back at least to the Greek philosopher Democritus – that all of what we see is an agglomeration of these underlying atomic elements. So a flower might be seen as consisting of a long, thin, vertical tubular base extending up into flat, rounded protrusions – well, you get the idea. The structuralists came up with these now seemingly strange analyses by the method of introspection – analyzing your own thought patterns in order to study as intensively and objectively as possible what it is you are thinking.

Later, psychologists in the *Gestalt* movement rebelled against the idea that our perceptions could be broken down into elementary atomic elements, and argued instead that the whole of what we perceive is greater than the sum of its parts. They scoffed at the idea that what we see is some kind of geometric panoply of forms and figures. Instead, they argued that no decomposition of a flower would ever capture what makes it so beautiful, so special, and so desirable to us.

The Gestaltists used experimental methods to develop and test their ideas rather than the introspection of the structuralists.

Eventually, psychologists with a *cognitive* perspective would combine the structuralists' emphasis on decomposition with empirical methods closer to those of the Gestaltists to try to understand how people perceive, learn, and think. The cognitive way of seeing things – understanding the underlying structures and processes of thought – became very popular in psychology, and cognitivism came to affect not only the study of perception and thinking, but diverse fields such as personality and social psychology as well.

Cognitivism, which is still popular today, views the mind as a super-sophisticated computer. Some cognitivists emphasize the step-by-step nature of human thinking, others the fact that many operations can occur simultaneously or in parallel. But the use of the computer metaphor unites almost all of them. And as in the past, psychologists such as Philip Johnson-Laird have argued that today's metaphor is the final one – that now we understand how the mind works.[6]

There have also been many critiques of the computer metaphor.[7] My goal is not to repeat them here, but to consider whether those interested in styles are well served by a computer metaphor, in contrast to the governmental metaphor. The computer metaphor seems like a good contrast, because it is so widely used today not only in the study of cognition, but also in the study of personality. And styles are a construct that can be placed at the interface between cognition and personality.

CONCLUSIONS

Styles matter. Moreover, they are often confused with abilities, so that students or others are thought to be incompetent not because they are lacking in abilities, but because their styles of thinking do not match those of the people doing the assessments. Especially in teaching, we need to take into account students' styles of thinking if we hope to reach them.

We need to consider carefully how our practices in educational settings may deprive able people of opportunities, while giving opportunities to those who are less able. For example, extensive use of multiple-choice testing in the United States clearly benefits executive thinkers. Many tests of scholastic aptitude and other aptitudes confound measurements of styles with measurements of abilities. But replacing all of these tests with projects and portfolios would simply result in a different group of students being benefited. Ideally, we need to teach and assess to a variety of styles.

The same principle applies in the world of work. Almost all jobs require an interview. But an interview, like any other form of assessment, tends to benefit people with certain styles at the expense of people with other styles. You will do better in an interview if you are external, and thus relate more readily and comfortably to your interviewer; hierarchical, and can thus get the main points about yourself into the interview in a short amount of time; and global enough to make sure that the interviewer gets the big picture about what you have to offer. This is not to say that there are no jobs for which these styles would not be beneficial. But these styles are not ideally suited to all jobs, so that the interview may be a better or worse selection device, depending on what it is being used for. Certainly, in the world of college admissions, it tends to favor a small subset of students over others who may be equally able.

Fortunately, some occupations allow flexibility in styles. For example, someone who wants to be a scholar might go into scientific research, which is more legislative, or into literary criticism, which is more judicial. Teachers may find themselves switching into the executive mode for many administrative jobs. Lawyers can become judges, giving themselves an opportunity to think in a more judicial way. So the world of work is sometimes tailored to allow people to express their stylistic preferences without changing career paths altogether. But such changes are not always possible, so that people need to think through what they do: An editor may be missing the chance to be a novelist, or vice versa.

So-called gifted adults are probably, in large part, those whose styles match their patterns of abilities. For example, someone with creative ability who has a legislative style will be at a distinct advantage over someone lacking in creative ability who also has a legislative style. On the other hand, someone who is a strong analytic thinker may find a judicial style more suited to analytical ability than would be a legislative style. To succeed, you need to find compatibility between how you think and how you think well.

In sum, we need to take styles into account in the worlds of education and work, and the theory of mental self-government provides a way to do so. If we don't take styles into account, we risk sacrificing some of our best talent to our confused notions of what it means to be smart or a high achiever, when in fact some of the smartest people and potentially highest achievers may only lack the style that we just happen to prefer.

Notes

CHAPTER 1. WHAT ARE THINKING STYLES AND
WHY DO WE NEED THEM?

1. Sternberg, R. J. (1985). Implicit theories of intelligence, creativity, and wisdom. *Journal of Personality and Social Psychology, 49,* 607–627.
2. Means, B., & Knapp, M. S. (1991). Cognitive approaches to teaching advanced skills to educationally disadvantaged children. *Phi Delta Kappan, 73,* 105–108.
3. Harris, K. R., & Marks, M. B. (1992). But good strategy instructors are constructivists! *Educational Psychology Review, 4,* 3–31.
4. Herrnstein, R., & Murray, C. (1994). *The bell curve.* New York: Free Press.
5. Sternberg, R. J. (1982). Teaching scientific thinking to gifted children. *Roeper Review, 4,* 4–6.
   Sternberg, R. J. (1982, April). Who's intelligent? *Psychology Today, 16,* 30–39.
   Sternberg, R. J. (1988). Mental self-government: A theory of intellectual styles and their development. *Human Development, 31,* 197–224.
   Sternberg, R. J. (1988). *The triarchic mind: A new theory of human intelligence.* New York: Viking.
   Sternberg, R. J. (1994). Thinking styles and testing: Bridging the gap between ability and personality assessment. In R. J. Sternberg & P. Ruzgis (Eds.), *Intelligence and personality.* New York: Cambridge University Press.

CHAPTER 2. FUNCTIONS OF THINKING STYLES: THE LEGISLATIVE, EXECUTIVE, AND JUDICIAL STYLES

1. Sternberg, R. J., & Wagner, R. K. (1991). *MSG Thinking Styles Inventory.* Unpublished manual.

CHAPTER 3. FORMS OF THINKING STYLES: THE MONARCHIC, HIERARCHIC, OLIGARCHIC, AND ANARCHIC STYLE

1. Poe, E. A. (1979). The tell-tale heart. In *Tales of Edgar Allan Poe* (p. 179). Franklin Center, PA: Franklin Library. (Original work published 1843.)
2. Poe, E. A. (1959). "For Annie." In *Poe* (p. 107). New York: Dell.

CHAPTER 4. LEVELS, SCOPE, AND LEANINGS OF THINKING STYLES: THE GLOBAL, LOCAL, INTERNAL, EXTERNAL, LIBERAL, AND CONSERVATIVE STYLES

1. Blum, M. L., & Naylor, J. C. (1968). *Industrial psychology, its theoretical and social foundation* (rev. ed.). New York: Harper & Row.
2. Williams, W. M., & Sternberg, R. J. (1988). Group intelligence: Why some groups are better than others. *Intelligence, 12,* 351–377.

CHAPTER 5. THE PRINCIPLES OF THINKING STYLES

1. Sternberg, R. J., & Lubart, T. I. (1995). *Defying the crowd: Cultivating creativity in a culture of conformity.* New York: Free Press.
2. Ibid.
3. Chapman, L. J., & Chapman, J. P. (1969). Illusory correlation as an obstacle to the use of valid psychodiagnostic signs. *Journal of Abnormal Psychology, 74,* 271–280.
4. Ceci, S. J. (1996). *On intelligence . . . more or less: A bio-ecological treatise on intellectual development.* Englewood Cliffs, NJ: Prentice-Hall.
   Gardner, H. (1983). *Frames of mind: The theory of multiple intelligences.* New York: Basic Books.
   Gardner, H. (1993). *Multiple intelligences: The theory in practice.* New York: Basic Books.
   Sternberg, R. J. (1985). *Beyond IQ: A triarchic theory of human intelligence.* New York: Cambridge University Press.

Sternberg, R. J. (1988). Intelligence. In R. J. Sternberg & E. E. Smith (Eds.), *The psychology of human thought*. New York: Cambridge University Press.

CHAPTER 6. THE DEVELOPMENT OF THINKING STYLES

1. Sternberg, R. J., & Suben, J. (1986). The socialization of intelligence. In M. Perlmutter (Ed.), *Perspectives on intellectual development: Minnesota symposia on child psychology* (Vol. 19, pp. 201–235). Hillsdale, NJ: Erlbaum.
2. Hofstede, G. (1980). *Culture's consequences*. Beverly Hills, CA: Sage.
   Kluckholn, F., & Strodtbeck, F. (1961). *Variation in value orientations*. Evanston, IL: Row, Peterson.
   Triandis, H. C. (1972). *The analysis of subjective culture*. New York: Wiley.
3. Matsumoto, D. (1996). *Culture and psychology*. Belmont, CA: Brooks/ Cole.
4. Hofstede, G. (1980). *Culture's consequences*. Beverly Hills, CA: Sage.
5. Berry, J. W., Poortinga, Y. H., Segall, M. H., & Dasen, P. R. (1992). *Cross-cultural psychology: Research and applications*. New York: Cambridge University Press.
6. Maryanne Martin, 1995. Personal communication.
7. Stanley, J. C., & Benbow, C. P. (1986). Youths who reason exceptionally well mathematically. In R. J. Sternberg & J. E. Davidson (Eds.), *Conceptions of giftedness* (pp. 361–387). New York: Cambridge University Press.
8. Sternberg, R. J., & Lubart, T. I. (1995). *Defying the crowd: Cultivating creativity in a culture of conformity*. New York: Free Press.
9. Ibid.
10. Sternberg, R. J. (1994). Answering questions and questioning answers. *Phi Delta Kappan, 76*(2), 136–138.
11. Sternberg, R. J. (1986). *Intelligence applied: Understanding and increasing your intellectual skills*. San Diego: Harcourt Brace Jovanovich.
12. Sternberg, R. J. (1996). *Successful intelligence*. New York: Simon & Schuster.
13. Ibid.

CHAPTER 7. THINKING STYLES IN THE CLASSROOM: WHAT HAVE WE LEARNED?

1. Spear, L. C., & Sternberg, R. J. (1987). Teaching styles: Staff development for teaching thinking. *Journal of Staff Development, 8*(3), 35–39.
2. Johnson, D. W., & Johnson, R. (1985). Classroom conflict: Controversy over debate in learning groups. *American Educational Research Journal, 22,* 237–256.

Slavin, R. E. (1994). *Cooperative learning* (2nd ed.). Boston: Allyn & Bacon.

3. Sternberg, R. J. (1994). Thinking styles: Theory and assessment at the interface between intelligence and personality. In R. J. Sternberg and P. Ruzgis (Eds.), *Intelligence and personality* (pp. 169–187). New York: Cambridge University Press.

   Sternberg, R. J., & Wagner, R. K. (1991). *MSG Thinking Styles Inventory.* Unpublished manual.

4. Sternberg, R. J. (1994). Allowing for thinking styles. *Educational Leadership, 52* (3), 36–40.

   Sternberg, R. J., & Grigorenko, E. L. (1993). Thinking styles and the gifted. *Roeper Review, 16*(2), 122–130.

   Sternberg, R. J., & Grigorenko, E. L. (1995). Styles of thinking in school. *European Journal of High Ability, 6*(2), 1–18.

   Sternberg, R. J., & Grigorenko, E. L. (1995). Thinking styles. In D. Saklofske & M. Zeidner (Eds.), *International handbook of personality and intelligence* (pp. 205–229). New York: Plenum.

5. Simonton, D. K. (1988). *Scientific genius.* New York: Cambridge University Press.

6. Grigorenko, E. L. , & Sternberg, R. J. (1997). Styles of thinking, abilities, and academic performance. *Exceptional Children, 63,* 295–312.

7. Sternberg, R. J. (1993). *Beyond IQ: A triarchic theory of human intelligence.* New York: Cambridge University Press.

   Sternberg, R. J. (1988). *The triarchic mind: A new theory of human intelligence.* New York: Viking.

   Sternberg, R. J. (1993). *Sternberg Triarchic Abilities Test.* Unpublished.

CHAPTER 8. A CAPSULE HISTORY OF THEORY AND RESEARCH ON STYLES

1. Goleman, D. (1995). *Emotional intelligence.* New York: Bantam.
   Salovey, P., & Mayer, J. D. (1990). Emotional intelligence. *Imagination, Cognition and Personality, 9*(3), 185–211.

2. Sternberg, R. J. (1985). *Beyond IQ: A triarchic theory of human intelligence.* New York: Cambridge University Press.

3. Witkin, H. A. (1973). *The role of cognitive style in academic performance and in teacher–student relations.* Unpublished report, Educational Testing Service, Princeton, NJ.

4. In the older Rod and Frame Test (RFT), the individual must ignore a visual context in order to locate a true vertical. In particular, a rod must be oriented

vertically with respect to the ground rather than to a frame that is situated at an angle with respect to the ground. Because the room is dark except for the lighted frame and rod, and because the person is seated at the same angle as the frame, the person cannot use the ground as a visual context cue. Thus, the person must ignore the distracting context (field) of the frame in order to locate the rod properly relative to the true vertical. See Witkin, H. A., Dyk, R. B., Faterson, H. F., Goodenough, D. R., & Karp, S. A. (1962). *Psychological differentiation.* New York: Wiley.

In the Embedded Figures Test (EFT), the test taker must locate a previously seen simple figure within a larger, more complex figure that has been designed to obscure or embed the simpler figure. This is a testlike analogue of the situations involving the earrings and the camouflage. See Witkin, H. A., & Oltman, P. K. (1972). *Manual for the Embedded Figures Test.* Palo Alto: Consulting Psychologists Press.

The field-independent person is able to locate the true vertical, despite the position of the frame, and to locate the embedded figures. The field-dependent person has more trouble with these tasks, presumably because he or she experiences the field of vision as more fused, so that it is difficult to separate one particular object from the field in which it is placed.

5. Witkin, H. A. (1973). *The role of cognitive style in academic performance and in teacher–student relations.* Unpublished report, Educational Testing Service, Princeton, NJ.

6. Goldstein, K. M., & Blackman, S. (1978). *Cognitive style.* New York: Wiley.

7. MacLeod, C. M., Jackson, R. A., & Palmer, J. (1986). On the relation between spatial ability and field dependence. *Intelligence, 10*(2), 141–151.

8. Gardner, R. W. (1953). Cognitive style in categorizing behavior. *Perceptual and Motor Skills, 22,* 214–233.
   Gardner, R. W. (1959). Cognitive control principles and perceptual behavior. *Bulletin of the Menninger Clinic, 23,* 241–248.
   Gardner, R. W. (1962). Cognitive controls in adaptation: Research and measurement. In S. Messick & J. Ross (Eds.), *Measurement in personality and cognition.* New York: Wiley.
   Gardner, R. W., Jackson, D. N., & Messick, S. J. (1960). Personality organization in cognitive controls and intellectual abilities. *Psychological Issues, 2*(4), 7.

9. The Free Sorting Test has been used to measure equivalence range. In the test, people are given the names of 73 common objects and are instructed to sort into groups the objects that seem to belong together. Those objects that do not seem to belong with any others can be placed into groups by themselves. The subject's score is the total number of groups formed, with lower

scores implying broader equivalence range and higher scores implying narrower equivalence range. Other scores can be derived as well. See Gardner, R. W. (1953). Cognitive style in categorizing behavior. *Perceptual and Motor Skills, 22,* 214–233.

10. Ceci, S. J. (1996). *On intelligence: A bio-ecological treatise on intellectual development* (expanded edition). Cambridge, MA: Harvard University Press.
   Streufert, S., & Streufert, S. C. (1978). *Behavior in the complex environment.* Washington, DC: Winston.

11. Gardner, R. W., & Schoen, R. A. (1962). Differentiation and abstraction in concept formation. *Psychological Monographs, 76.*
   Pettigrew, T. F. (1958). The measurement of category width as a cognitive variable. *Journal of Personality, 26,* 532–544.

12. Ibid.

13. Glixman, A. F. (1965). Categorizing behavior as a function of meaning domain. *Journal of Personality and Social Psychology, 2*(3), 370–377.
   Palei, A. I. (1986). Modal'nostnaya structura emotsional'nosti i cognitiv-nyi stil' (Russian). [Emotionality and cognitive style]. *Voprosy Psikhologii, 4,* 118–126.

14. Jerome Kagan and his colleagues' Conceptual Style Test (CST) is supposed to measure not right answers, but rather one of three "conceptual styles." The difference between the test and the rendition here is that here I am using words to describe objects, whereas the test uses pictures. See Kagan, J., Joss, H. A., & Sigel, I. G. (1963). Psychological significance of styles of conceptualization. *Monographs of the Society for Research in Child Development.* Chicago: University of Chicago Press.
   People with an *analytic-descriptive* style tend to group together pictures on the basis of common elements (e.g., airplane and bird because they both have wings, or two people who are both wearing socks). People with a *relational* style tend to group things together because of functional, thematic relations (e.g., both whales and sharks swim). People with an *inferential-categorical* style tend to group objects together because of an abstract similarity that can be inferred but usually not directly observed in the picture (e.g., both a whale and a tiger are mammals).
   As a measure, the CST is probably confounded with abilities. Indeed, in most theories of cognitive development, inferential-categorical thinking, as defined here, is seen as more sophisticated than is relational thinking, which is in turn seen as more sophisticated than what the theorists here call the analytic-descriptive style.
   For example, on the vocabulary tests of the Wechsler or the Stanford-

Binet intelligence scales, more credit is given for a categorical than for a functional definition. Thus, a child who defines an automobile as a vehicle of conveyance will receive more credit than will one who defines the automobile as something that uses gasoline. Similarly, in the theory of Jean Piaget, a child is viewed as cognitively more advanced if he or she can use formal operations (logical thinking) than if he or she can only see concrete relations between things of the kind required by, say, the descriptive style. See Piaget, J. (1972). *The psychology of intelligence*. Totowa, NJ: Littlefield Adams.

15. Kagan, J. (1958). The concept of identification. *Psychological Review, 65,* 296–305.

Kagan, J. (1965). Impulsive and reflective children: Significance of conceptual tempo. In J. D. Krumboltz (Ed.), *Learning and the educational process* (pp. 133–161). Chicago: Rand McNally.

Kagan, J. (1966). Reflection–impulsivity: The generality and dynamics of conceptual tempo. *Journal of Abnormal Psychology, 71,* 17–27.

16. The test most frequently used to measure impulsivity versus reflectivity, the Matching Familiar Figures Test (MFFT), requires people to select, from among several alternatives, the picture that exactly matches a standard picture. Test takers are measured both for how quickly they finish the test and for the number of errors they make.

See Block, J., Block, J. H., & Harrington, D. M. (1974). Some misgivings about the Matching Familiar Figures Test as a measure of reflection–impulsivity. *Developmental Psychology, 11,* 611–632.

Butter, E. (1979) Visual and haptic training on cross-model transfer of reflectivity. *Journal of Educational Psychology, 72,* 212–219.

Kagan, J. (1966). Reflection–impulsivity: The generality and dynamics of conceptual tempo. *Journal of Abnormal Psychology, 71,* 17–24.

The rationale of the MFFT is that impulsive people will tend to complete many problems, but with a relatively high error rate; reflective people will tend to complete fewer problems, but with a relatively low error rate. Two other categories of scorers, of less interest to cognitive-styles researchers, are those who finish many items accurately (who are labeled as quick) and those who finish few items but make a lot of errors nevertheless (who are labeled as slow). See Eska, B., & Black, K. N. (1971). Conceptual tempo in young grade-school children. *Child Development, 45,* 505–516.

This test, like the Embedded Figures Test, has the feeling of an ability test, and indeed, its content is practically identical to that found on certain tests of perceptual-motor or clerical ability. What distinguishes this test from the abilities tests is the type of data of interest. Here, the investigator is interested in the pattern of response times versus error rates, and looks only at people who trade off accuracy for speed in one way or another. The quick and slow people are not exhibiting a cognitive style at all, but rather a skill. Whether the same test is well used when it measures both abilities and styles is an open question, but such a test certainly seems on its face to be nonideal.

Although there seem to be relations between impulsivity–reflectivity and various personality attributes, the kind of impulsivity measured by the MFFT appears to be different from the kind of impulsivity measured by personality tests. See Furnham, M. J., & Kendall, P. C. (1986). Cognitive tempo and behavioral adjustment in children. *Cognitive Therapy and Research, 10*, 45–50. For example, one study found that scores on the test were related to attentional deficit, but not to any of 11 other behavioral problems, including aggressiveness, social withdrawal, and delinquency, among other attributes. See Achenbach, T. M., & Edelbrocker, C. (1983). *Manual for the Child Behavior Checklist and Revised Child Behavior Profile.* Burlington, VT: Department of Psychiatry, University of Vermont.

17. Bryant, N., & Gettinger, M. (1981). Eliminating differences between learning disabled and nondisabled children on a paired-associate learning task. *Journal of Educational Research, 74*, 342–346.

Camara, R. P. S., & Fox, R. (1983). Impulsive versus inefficient problem solving in retarded and nonretarded Mexican children. *Journal of Psychology, 114*(2), 187–191.

Eska, B., & Black, K. N. (1971). Conceptual tempo in young grade-school children. *Child Development, 45*, 505–516.

Stahl, S. A, Erickson, L. G., & Rayman, M. C. (1986). Detection of inconsistencies by reflective and impulsive seventh-grade readers. *National Reading Conference Yearbook, 35*, 233–238.

Zelniker, T., & Oppenheimer, L. (1973). Modification of information processing of impulsive children. *Child Development, 44*, 445–450.

18. Kagan, J. (1966). Reflection–impulsivity: The generality and dynamics of conceptual tempo. *Journal of Abnormal Psychology, 71*, 17–27.

Messer, S. (1970). The effect of anxiety over intellectual performance on reflection–impulsivity in children. *Child Development, 41*, 353–359.

Paulsen, K. (1978). Reflection–impulsivity and level of maturity. *Journal of Psychology, 99*, 109–112.

19. Messick, S., & Kogan, N. (1963). Differentiation and compartmentalization in object-sorting measures of categorizing style. *Perceptual and Motor Skills, 16*, 47–51.

20. Harvey, O. J., Hunt, D. E., & Schroder, H. M. (1961) *Conceptual systems and personality organization.* New York: Wiley.

21. Feuerstein, R. (1979). *The dynamic assessment of retarded performers: The learning potential assessment device, theory, instruments, and techniques.* Baltimore: University Park Press.

22. Klein, G. S., & Schlesinger, H. J. (1951). Perceptual attitudes toward instability: I. Prediction of apparent movement experiences from Rorschach responses. *Journal of Personality, 19,* 289–302.

23. Gardner, R. W., & Moriarty, A. (1968). Dimensions of cognitive control at preadolescence. In R. Gardner (Ed.), *Personality development at preadolescence.* Seattle: University of Washington Press.

24. Sternberg, R. J., & Ruzgis, P. (Eds.) (1994). *Personality and intelligence.* New York: Cambridge University Press.

25. Kogan, N. (1973). Creativity and cognitive style: A life-span perspective. In P. B. Baltes & K. W. Schaie (Eds.), *Life-span developmental psychology: Personality and socialization* (pp. 145–178). New York: Academic Press.

26. Jung, C. G. (1923). *Psychological types.* New York: Harcourt Brace.
    Myers, I. B., & Myers, P. B. (1980). *Manual: A guide to use of the Myers-Briggs Type Indicator.* Palo Alto, CA: Consulting Psychologists Press.

27. Grigorenko, E. L., & Sternberg, R. J. (1995). Thinking styles. In D. Saklofske & M. Zeidner (Eds.), *International handbook of personality and intelligence* (pp. 205–229). New York: Plenum.
    Myers, I. B. (1980). *Gifts differing.* Palo Alto, CA: Consulting Psychologists Press.
    Myers, I. B., & McCaulley, M. H. (1985). *Manual: A guide to the development and use of the Myers-Briggs Type Indicator.* Palo Alto, CA: Consulting Psychologists Press.
    Myers, I. B., & Myers, P. B. (1980). *Manual: A guide to use of the Myers-Briggs Type Indicator.* Palo Alto, CA: Consulting Psychologists Press.

28. Styles in this theory are measured via the Myers-Briggs Type Indicator, or MBTI, which is a published and widely available test that looks a lot like a personality inventory. People respond to statements about themselves in a way that ultimately classifies them as belonging to one category or another. See Myers, I. B., & McCaulley, M. H. (1985). *Manual: A guide to the development and use of the Myers-Briggs Type Indicator.* Palo Alto, CA: Consulting Psychologists Press.

29. Bargar, R. R., & Hoover, R. L. (1984). Psychological type and the matching of cognitive styles. *Theory into Practice, 23,* 1, 56–63.
    Corman, L. S., & Platt, R. G. (1988). Correlations among the Group Embedded Figures Test, the Myers-Briggs Type Indicator and demographic characteristics: A business school study. *Perceptual and Motor Skills, 66(2),* 507–511.
    Hennessy, S. M. (1992). *A study of uncommon Myers-Briggs cognitive*

styles in law enforcement. Dissertation Abstracts International, *52*(12-A), 4308.

30. Gregorc, A. F. (1979). Learning/teaching styles: Potent forces behind them. *Educational Leadership, 36*(4), 234–236.
Gregorc, A. F. (1982). *Gregorc style delineator.* Maynard, MA: Gabriel Systems.
Gregorc, A. F. (1984). Style as a symptom: A phenomenological perspective. *Theory Into Practice. 23*(1), 51–55.
Gregorc, A. F. (1985). *Inside styles: Beyond the basics.* Maynard, MA: Gabriel Systems.

31. Goldsmith, R. E. (1985). The factorial composition of the KAI Inventory. *Educational and Psychological Measurement, 45,* 245–250.
Joniak, A. J., & Isaksen, S. G. (1988). The Gregorc Style Delineator: Internal consistency and its relationship to Kirton's adaptive-innovative distinction. *Educational and Psychological Measurement, 8,* 1043–1049.
Keller, R. T., & Holland, W. E. (1978). A cross-validation of the KAI in three research and development organizations. *Applied Psychological Measurement, 2,* 563–570.
Kirton, M. J., & de Ciantis, S. M. (1986). Cognitive styles and personality. The Kirton's Adaption-Innovation and Cattell's 16 Personality Factor Inventory. *Personality and Individual Differences 7(2),* 141–146.
Mulligan, D. G., & Martin, W. (1980). Adaptors, innovators and promises in educational practice. *Educational Psychologist, 19,* 59–74.
O'Brien, T. P. (1990). Construct validation of the Gregorc Style Delineator: An application of Lisrel 7. *Educational and Psychological Measurement, 50,* 631–636.
Ross, J. (1962). Factor analysis and levels of measurement in psychology. In S. Messick & J. Ross (Eds.), *Measurement in personality and cognition.* New York: Wiley.

32. Kolb, D. A. (1974). On management and the learning process. In D. A. Kolb, I. M. Rubin, & J. M. McIntyre (Eds.), *Organizational psychology.* Englewood Cliffs, NJ: Prentice-Hall.

33. Kolb, D. A. (1978). *Learning Style Inventory technical manual.* Boston: McBer & Co.

34. Dunn, R., & Dunn, K. (1978). *Teaching students through their individual learning styles.* Reston, VA: Reston Publishing.
Dunn, R., Dunn, K., & Price, K. (1979). *Learning Style Inventory (LSI) for students in grades 3–12.* Reston, VA: National Association of Secondary School Principals.

35. Holland, J. L. (1973). *Making vocational choices: A theory of careers.* Englewood Cliffs, NJ: Prentice-Hall.
36. Henson, K. T., & Borthwick, P. (1984). Matching styles: A historical look. *Theory into Practice, 23,* 1, 3–9, 31.

CHAPTER 9. WHY A THEORY OF MENTAL SELF-GOVERNMENT?

1. Tourangeau, R., & Sternberg, R. J. (1981). Aptness in metaphor. *Cognitive Psychology, 13,* 27–55.
2. Ford, M. E. (1986). A living systems conceptualization of social intelligence: Outcomes, processes, and developmental change. In R. J. Sternberg (Ed.), *Advances in the psychology of human intelligence* (Vol. 3). Hillsdale, NJ: Erlbaum.
   Kauffman, S. (1995). *At home in the universe.* New York: Oxford University Press.
3. Ford, M. E. (1986). A living systems conceptualization of social intelligence: Outcomes, processes, and developmental change. In R. J. Sternberg (Ed.), *Advances in the psychology of human intelligence* (Vol. 3). Hillsdale, NJ: Erlbaum.
   Ford, M. E. (1994). A living systems approach to the integration of personality and intelligence. In R. J. Sternberg and P. Ruzgis (Eds.), *Personality and intelligence* (pp. 188–217). New York: Cambridge University Press.
   Plomin, R. (1990). *Nature and nurture: An introduction to human behavioral genetics* Pacific Grove, CA: Brooks/Cole.
   Sternberg, R. J. (1985). *Beyond IQ: A triarchic theory of human intelligence.* New York: Cambridge University Press.
4. Ford, M. E. (1994). A living systems approach to the integration of personality and intelligence. In R. J. Sternberg and P. Ruzgis (Eds.), *Personality and intelligence* (pp. 188–217). New York: Cambridge University Press.
   Plomin, R. (1988). The nature and nurture of cognitive abilities. In R. J. Sternberg (Ed.), *Advances in the psychology of human intelligence* (Vol. 4, pp. 1–33). Hillsdale, NJ: Erlbaum.
   Sternberg, R. J. (1990). *Metaphors of mind: Conceptions of the nature of intelligence.* New York: Cambridge University Press.
5. Hegel, G. W. F. (1931). *The phenomenology of mind* (2d ed.; J. B. Baillie, Trans.). London: Allen & Unwin. (Original work published 1807).
   Sternberg, R. J. (1995). *In search of the human mind.* Orlando: Harcourt Brace College Publishers.

6. Johnson-Laird, P. N. (1988). *The computer and the mind.* Cambridge, MA: Harvard University Press.
   Johnson-Laird, P. N. (1989). Freedom and constraint in creativity. In R. J. Sternberg (Ed.), *The nature of creativity* (pp. 202–219). New York: Cambridge University Press.
7. Searle, J. R. (1980). Minds, brains, and programs. *Behavioral and Brain Sciences, 3,* 417–424.

Index